Ask your fellow cadets to sign your Yearbook, then save it as a keepsake for the future

ARMY CADET YEARBOOK

ARMY CADET YEARBOOK

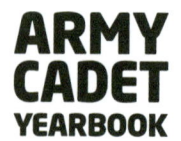

Army Cadets' commissioning editors: Charley Doyle and Adam Simmonds

Editor: Rosanna Rothery

Editorial team: Kathryn Lewis, Abi Manning,
Melissa Morris, Kirstie Newton, Jo Rees, Melissa Stewart and Selena Young

Design: Samuel Freeman, Wroxy Meredith,
Chrissy Mouncey and Dale Stiling

Production: Tamsin Powell

armycadets.com

ISBN 978-1-7391668-4-7

First published in Great Britain in 2023 by Army Cadets UK

Text © Crown Copyright – Army Cadets 2023

Design and layout © Crown Copyright – Army Cadets 2023

Printed in Great Britain

salt

saltmedia.co.uk

01271 859299   ideas@saltmedia.co.uk

The right of Army Cadets UK to be identified as the author of this work has been asserted by it in accordance with the Copyright, Designs and Patents Act 1988.

A catalogue record of the book is available from the British Library.

All rights reserved. No part of this publication may be reproduced, distributed, or transmitted in any form or by any means, including photocopying, recording, or other electronic or mechanical methods, without the prior written permission of the publisher, except in the case of brief quotations embodied in critical reviews and certain other non-commercial uses permitted by copyright law.

For permission requests, contact armycadets.com

While every effort has been made to ensure the accuracy of the information in this publication, we cannot be held responsible for any errors or omissions and take no responsibility for the consequences of error or for any loss or damage suffered by users of any of the information published on any of these pages.

While all information is considered to be true and correct at the date of publication, changes in circumstances after the time of publication may impact on the accuracy of the information.

FSC
www.fsc.org
MIX
Paper from responsible sources
FSC® C019670

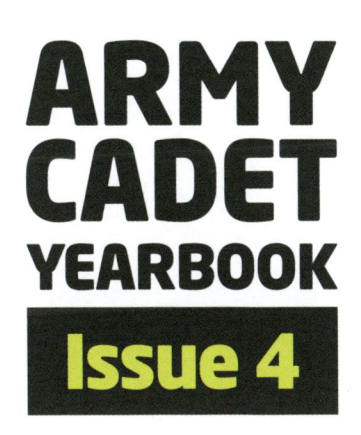

ARMY CADET YEARBOOK
Issue 4

'I hope to meet as many of you as possible over the coming months as, together, we deliver the ultimate Army Cadets experience'

Welcome

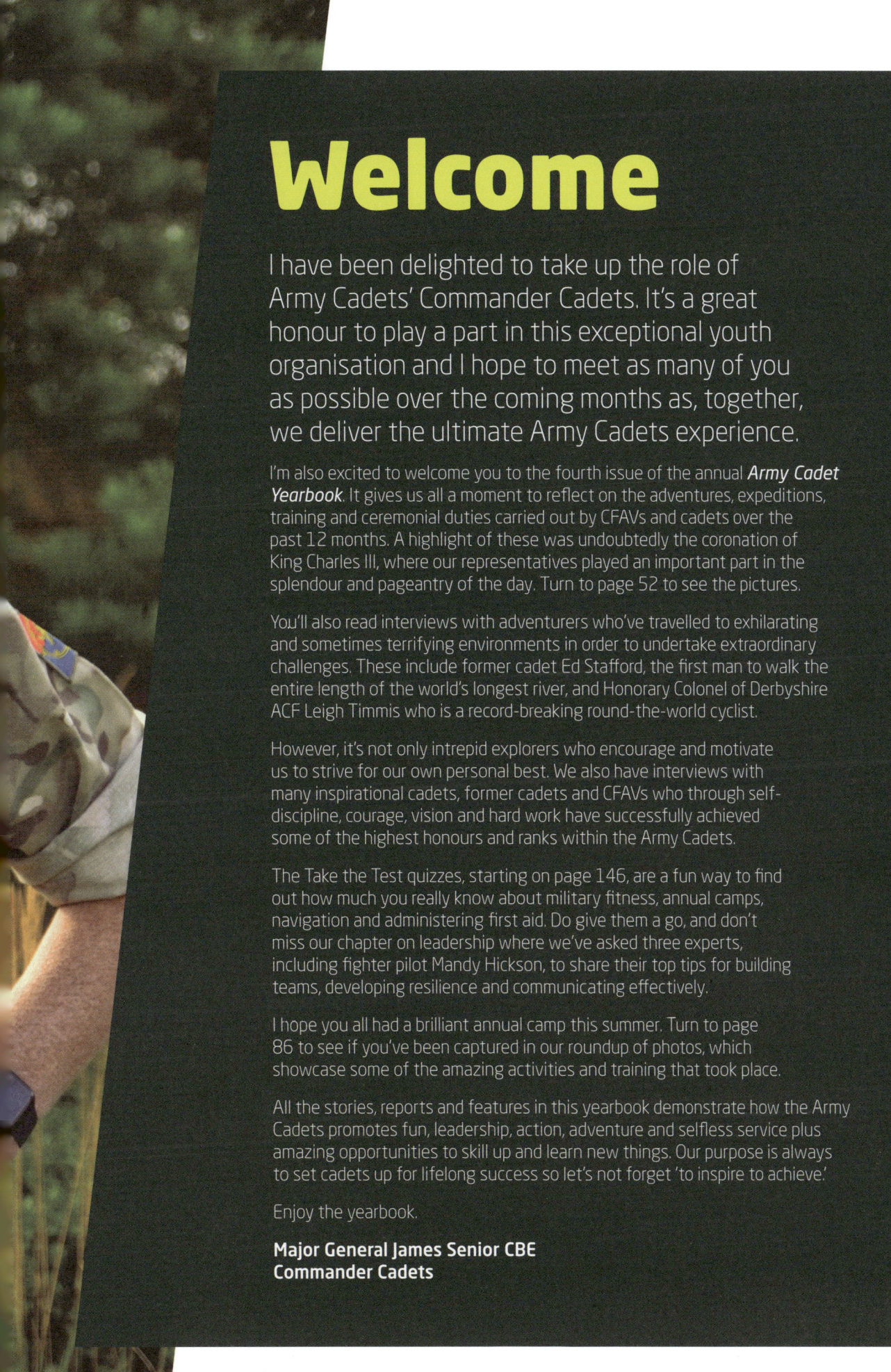

I have been delighted to take up the role of Army Cadets' Commander Cadets. It's a great honour to play a part in this exceptional youth organisation and I hope to meet as many of you as possible over the coming months as, together, we deliver the ultimate Army Cadets experience.

I'm also excited to welcome you to the fourth issue of the annual ***Army Cadet Yearbook***. It gives us all a moment to reflect on the adventures, expeditions, training and ceremonial duties carried out by CFAVs and cadets over the past 12 months. A highlight of these was undoubtedly the coronation of King Charles III, where our representatives played an important part in the splendour and pageantry of the day. Turn to page 52 to see the pictures.

You'll also read interviews with adventurers who've travelled to exhilarating and sometimes terrifying environments in order to undertake extraordinary challenges. These include former cadet Ed Stafford, the first man to walk the entire length of the world's longest river, and Honorary Colonel of Derbyshire ACF Leigh Timmis who is a record-breaking round-the-world cyclist.

However, it's not only intrepid explorers who encourage and motivate us to strive for our own personal best. We also have interviews with many inspirational cadets, former cadets and CFAVs who through self-discipline, courage, vision and hard work have successfully achieved some of the highest honours and ranks within the Army Cadets.

The Take the Test quizzes, starting on page 146, are a fun way to find out how much you really know about military fitness, annual camps, navigation and administering first aid. Do give them a go, and don't miss our chapter on leadership where we've asked three experts, including fighter pilot Mandy Hickson, to share their top tips for building teams, developing resilience and communicating effectively.

I hope you all had a brilliant annual camp this summer. Turn to page 86 to see if you've been captured in our roundup of photos, which showcase some of the amazing activities and training that took place.

All the stories, reports and features in this yearbook demonstrate how the Army Cadets promotes fun, leadership, action, adventure and selfless service plus amazing opportunities to skill up and learn new things. Our purpose is always to set cadets up for lifelong success so let's not forget 'to inspire to achieve.'

Enjoy the yearbook.

Major General James Senior CBE
Commander Cadets

Contents

» **Welcome** — 6
　Army Cadets values — 12
　Message from our National Honorary Colonel — 14

» **Year in focus** — 16
　Cadets and the coronation — 52
　Celebrating CCF75 — 60

» **Adventurers** — 66
　Amazon adventurer Ed Stafford — 68
　Survival state of mind with Megan Hine — 72
　Riding highs with Leigh Timmis — 76
　Intrepid explorer Laura Bingham — 80

» **Annual camps** — 86

» **Inspiration** — 120
　The secretive world of the cyber-threat hunter — 122
　Meet entrepreneur Jeremiah Emmanuel BEM — 126
　TV's Dr Ranj Singh on finding your own amazing — 130
　Meet Somerset's lord-lieutenant's cadet — 134
　Champion Cadet Josh Siggers — 138
　What does it take to be a cadet regimental sergeant major? — 142

14

52

16

60

80

76

86

Contents

» **Take the test** — **146**
　Military fitness — 148
　First aid in freezing weather — 152
　Annual camp — 156
　Navigation — 160

» **Leadership** — **164**
　Fighter pilot Mandy Hickson on leadership — 166
　12 tips for authentic leadership — 170
　Sally Orange's seven ways to be more resilient — 174

» **Cadet life** — **178**
　Top exped tips — 180
　Decoding CyberFirst — 186
　First aid heroes — 190
　Hydration 101 — 196
　Spotlight on The Ulysses Trust — 198
　Spotlight on Army Cadet Charitable Trust UK — 202

» **Cadet Forces Medals** — **206**

142

148

198

190

Army Cadet Yearbook Issue 4

11

ARMY CADETS
VALUES

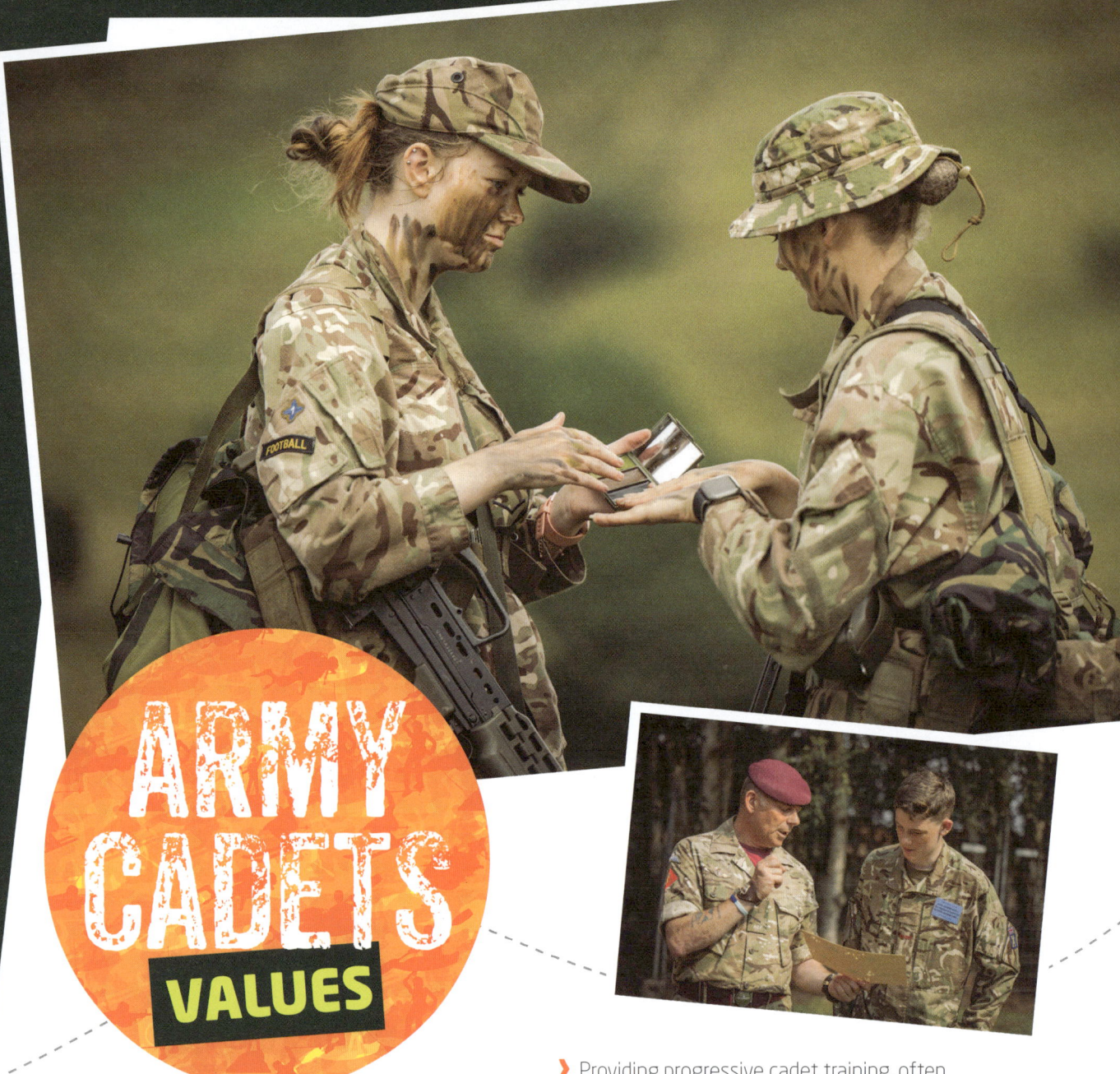

Army Cadets is a national voluntary youth organisation, sponsored by the Army to provide challenging military, adventurous and community activities.

Its aim is to inspire young people to achieve success in life with a spirit of service to the King, their country and their local community, and to help them become good citizens. This is achieved by:

❯ Providing progressive cadet training, often of a challenging and exciting nature, to foster confidence, self-reliance, initiative, loyalty and a sense of service to other people.

❯ Encouraging the development of personal powers of practical leadership and the ability to work successfully as a member of a team.

❯ Stimulating an interest in the Army and its achievements, skills and values.

❯ Advising and preparing those considering a career in the services or with the reserve forces.

OUR VALUES

» COURAGE

Courage is both physical and moral. Physical courage is what enables us to motivate others when the activity or the environment is hard or demanding, such as hiking across Dartmoor as part of a Ten Tors team. Moral courage is having the strength and confidence to do what is right even when it might make us unpopular, such as standing up to bullying. It is also the courage to insist on maintaining the highest standards of behaviour. Both physical and moral courage are equally important, and showing courage in all forms earns respect and fosters trust.

» DISCIPLINE

Discipline helps us all to work effectively as part of a team. It isn't just about being told off for doing something wrong; it's about having the self-control to not do the wrong thing, and the self-confidence to stand up to those who do.

Self-discipline is the ability to make the time to polish our boots, iron our uniform and be smart on parade, no matter what other distractions are around us.

Discipline helps build our team so everyone is trusted to do the task well. Good discipline means we all do the right thing – even when it's difficult.

» LOYALTY

Loyalty is what keeps teams together. In Army Cadets that team could be our detachment, county, section, contingent or any other team we are part of, such as on an expedition, overseas exchange or sports team.

When we work together in a team we achieve so much more. However, loyalty must only support positive behaviours and actions. Loyalty to a team should never allow poor behaviours or the wrong thing to be done. Letting others stray from our values is not loyal to the team.

» RESPECT FOR OTHERS

Respect for others means we treat others as we'd like to be treated.

Army Cadets is a very varied and mixed team, and we must not discriminate against anyone because of their gender or because they have a different ethnic background, religion or sexual orientation to us.

We recognise the value everyone brings to the team and that they all have different viewpoints and ways to contribute. We have respect for others, not only because it is a legal obligation but because teams that embrace difference and diversity are stronger.

» INTEGRITY

Integrity means being truthful and honest, and trusting those above us in the organisation.

When we show integrity we build trust in ourselves and in our team, and this makes the team stronger and able to do more.

Showing integrity also helps others outside Army Cadets trust us and helps us to do more in our communities. It's important that everyone, from the newest cadet to senior officers, demonstrates integrity in everything they do, otherwise trust will be eroded.

» SELFLESS COMMITMENT

Selfless commitment is critical to good leadership and teamwork. It is about putting the needs of others ahead of our own to help everyone succeed.

We demonstrate this when we help someone with a lesson they are finding difficult, rather than going off for a break, or when we hang back with someone who is struggling on an expedition, rather than speeding on ahead. Without selfless commitment we can't be good leaders. Remember the motto of Royal Military Academy Sandhurst, where Army officers are trained, is 'Serve to Lead'.

Message from our National Honorary Colonel

Lorraine Kelly CBE

The presenter, journalist and star of her own daytime TV show *Lorraine* reveals why she is proud to be the **Army Cadets' National Honorary Colonel**.

As Army Cadets' National Honorary Colonel, I am always thrilled to pick up the latest edition of the yearbook and read about the many inspiring acts of service carried out by cadets across the UK. These include taking part in Remembrance Day parades, raising substantial sums of money for good causes and heroically putting first-aid skills into practice in real-life situations. And this year, as always, I've been impressed by the courage, determination and self-discipline shown by our young people and the CFAVs who guide them.

Looking through the pages of this yearbook, I'm struck by the remarkable activities some of our cadets have experienced over the last year, including adventurous training trips, skiing expeditions, European battlefield tours, cultural exchanges with the USA and India, and learning how to parachute jump.

When asked about the Army Cadets by people outside the organisation I'm always keen to stress the wealth of opportunities it offers young people. Every cadet is able to try a diverse range of activities, which have the potential to become fulfilling hobbies while also positively impacting their self esteem, communication skills and resilience – exactly the qualities they'll need to navigate their future lives.

It's my hope that all cadets will take advantage of the many activities on offer and give them their all, whether that's learning to play an instrument with a view to joining a county band, working towards a DofE award, trying a new sport such as archery, rugby or cross country, or attending a STEM camp or CIS conference. There is so much to be gained in terms of making new friends, learning new skills and building confidence.

I'm particularly pleased to see a chapter of this book entirely devoted to leadership. These inspirational interviews aren't just relevant to cadets with ambitions to join the armed forces. Everyone should be able to communicate effectively, lead a team with confidence and show integrity and respect for others – whichever career path they follow.

Finally, a huge thank you to the CFAVs who selflessly commit so many hours ensuring cadets get a truly awesome experience. Your enthusiasm and commitment are inspirational!

Lorraine Kelly CBE
Army Cadets' National Honorary Colonel

LORRAINE KELLY

'It's my hope that all cadets will take advantage of the many activities on offer and give them their all'

YEAR IN FOCUS

Get the low-down on activities carried out by the Army Cadets during the last year and discover some of the events that took place, including the King's coronation and CCF75.

AUTUMN 2022

World Mental Health Day
10 October

Army Cadets' Healthy Minds campaign has led to great progress in the way Counties nurture mental health within the organisation. The initiative, rolled out through national training programmes since September 2020, breaks down barriers, reduces stigma and promotes mental health awareness.

In 2022, the Senior Cadet Healthy Minds facilitator course was launched at CTC Frimley Park. SO1 Medical and First Aid Mel Prangnell (pictured inset) said: *'We recognised that we needed to offer something to young people too, so we took the Mental Health Awareness course we developed for adults and adapted it for young people.*

'Senior cadets have the ability to help younger cadets because they can get alongside them and relate to their experiences. It also teaches senior cadets to lead by example.'

The course maintains a delicate balance between a senior cadet responding to a younger cadet's concerns while not taking responsibility themselves:

'Peer-to-peer support is fantastic, but we want to make sure cadets don't feel overly responsible for making sure other young people's mental health is OK.'

» Lancashire ACF leads the charge

Healthy Minds National Trainer Major Wenda Tyrer trialled the Senior Cadet Healthy Minds facilitator course during camp, as well as offering a quiet room for cadets who felt overwhelmed.

She has also implemented new initiatives around mental health and wellbeing within Lancashire ACF (pictured above). These include a wellbeing garden at their training centre, plus a wellbeing weekend retreat on a farm so cadets could feel the positive effects of being immersed in nature.

'The cadets in her County have benefitted from the new measures,' said Mel. *'It demonstrates a County trainer who is considering the cadet experience as a whole and has taken the Healthy Minds initiative and run with it.'*

To Inspire To Achieve

» Cadets' special relationship

CCF cadets from Royal Hospital School (RHS) in Suffolk enjoyed an exchange with cadets from the USA. American cadets from Georgia Military College (GMC) and the Riverside Military Academy (now Riverside Prepatory Academy) visited the UK in June and October.

During the October visit, US cadets took part in four days of fieldcraft training, which included living in the field on military rations, learning leadership skills, and carrying out teamwork in various tactical scenarios.

As well as visiting London, the US cadets took a trip to Cambridge where they went to the American Air Museum at the Imperial War Museum Duxford and the Cambridge American Cemetery and Memorial.

RHS cadets spent nearly three weeks in the summer with the American cadets in the US, participating in academic, sporting and cadet activities. These included foot drill, dynamic rifle drill and Raider (an athletic competition) training.

The mutual visits were part of the Ex UNITED CADET exchange programme, which centres around the commonality in cadet activity through the CCF and US Army Junior Reserve Officers' Training Corps (JROTC). The exchange provides cadets with an insight into the interdependence of nations and, in particular, the strong and special relationship between the US and the UK.

Above top: Cadets meet their American counterparts.
Above: CFAVs from both sides of the Atlantic.
Left: RMA cadets watch a divisions parade at RHS

AUTUMN 2022

Photos: Kate Knight

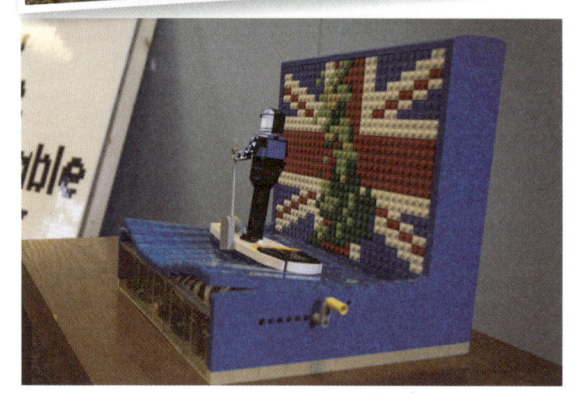

» Learning STEM with Lego

In October, Army Cadets National Ambassador Jordan Wylie and Steve Guinness (AKA The Brick Consultant) led a fun and creative Lego workshop at the Army Cadets STEM Camp at Westdown Camp, Salisbury. After listening to an inspirational talk from Jordan, cadets worked in teams to complete a mini Lego replica of his Great British Paddle stand-up paddleboard as well as a Lego ACCT UK logo.

The week-long camp (Ex STEM CHALLENGE), sponsored by ACCT UK, also included workshops and talks from adventurers Bernie Hollywood OBE and Paula Reid plus Jason Woodcock from Channel 4's *Hunted* and former RAF tornado pilot Mandy Hickson.

Over 250 cadets took part in the camp, where they watched a series of presentations and took part in hands-on challenges, all delivered by the Army's leading STEM experts in six specialised areas and based around some of the most high-tech military equipment in the world. Workshops demonstrated how the Army's advanced STEM technology uses many of the same principles that cadets learn in their lessons at school.

The aim of the camp was to enthuse cadets with a passion for STEM while encouraging them to think about how choosing science, technology, engineering and maths at school could lead to interesting and rewarding career options.

Top and middle: Cadets got up close to some of the most high-tech military equipment in the world. Bottom: A miniature Lego version of Jordan Wylie's Great British Paddle stand-up paddleboard and an ACCT UK logo

Photos: Kate Knight

» WW1 battlefield tour

Cadets from Black Watch Battalion ACF carried out research into members of their families who fought Ypres and Passchendaele before embarking on a five-day visit to Belgium and northern France.

During the October trip, cadets went to Ypres and the Somme. At the former, highlights included studying the Bayernwald German trench system, viewing life-size reconstructions of First World War battle scenes at the Hooge Crater Museum and attending the Last Post Ceremony at Menin Gate.

At the Somme, poignant moments were had at Newfoundland Memorial Park and the Thiepval Memorial to the Missing. One cadet wrote afterwards: *'This trip has given us peace that … many of our family members have a known and marked grave so they can be remembered.'*

» Half-term adventures

The autumn half term is always a busy time for the Army Cadets, and thousands of cadets attended all kinds of diverse and exciting events across the country. Some of the activities supported by ACCT UK included a National First Aid Competition at Holcombe Moor and Army Cadet Band Camps at Altcar and Longmoor.

Above: Lt Gina Allsop won The Inspiration Award for her fundraising. Below: Army Cadets National Ambassador Sally Orange won the Sporting Excellence Award

» Triple whammy for Army Cadets

Three stalwarts of the Army Cadets community were honoured at the Soldiering On Awards in London in October.

Army Cadets National Ambassador Sally Orange won the Sporting Excellence Award for her outstanding multiple Guinness World Records, world firsts and charity fundraising. Diversity and Inclusion Advisor for Army Cadets Scotland Lt Col Gilly Moncur was presented with a Special Recognition Award for her unstinting efforts to ensure Army Cadets is an inclusive and welcoming youth organisation. Lt Gina Allsop of Sussex ACF came away with The Inspiration Award for her relentless fundraising work for Army Cadets, SSAFA, Sporting Force and animal rescue charities.

They were joined by Colonel Cadets (East Midlands) 7 Brigade Leona Barr-Jones, who finally got the chance to celebrate face-to-face after her Defence Inclusivity Award win in 2020. The Soldiering On Awards recognise the outstanding achievements of those who have served in the Armed Forces as well those who work in support of the Armed Forces community.

Lt Col Gilly Moncur was presented with a Special Recognition Award

Photos: Robert Weiderman

» Subaquatic scholarships

Two cadets from Ash Manor CCF received an exciting four-year scholarship with the British Sub-Aqua Club (BSAC). **Cpl Beth** and **LCpl Mikyle** were granted a fantastic opportunity to learn to dive and become future instructors with BSAC.

The scholarship will take them from entry-level ocean diver to open water instructor, with BSAC providing the courses and Divecrew (leading scuba diving specialists) giving them practical training and experience.

Beth already has a keen interest in marine conservation and would like to dive with sharks and turtles in the future, while Mikyle would like to swim with sharks and see different varieties of life under the water. The two scholars were selected for this training opportunity by SERFCA (Reserve Forces' and Cadets' Association for the South East) and Divecrew. They will report on their progress and experiences so other cadets might be inspired to take up scuba diving training and discover more about the ocean environment.

Standing, left to right: Lt Chiara Bettis, Karen (mother of Cpl Beth), Mark Paisey (BSAC), Darya (father of LCpl Mikyle), WO2 Jim Chalmers. Seated, left to right: Cpl Beth and LCpl Mikyle

» Ex NORMANDY LANDING

In October, after three years of planning, cadets and CFAVs from both West Lowland and Glasgow & Lanarkshire Battalions ferried to France for a Second World War battlefield tour.

Visits to historic memorial sites, beaches, museums and battlefields proved to be a meaningful experience: *'The most memorable part of the trip was the Normandy American Cemetery,'* said Cdt Sgt Maj Scott Connor of Glasgow & Lanarkshire Battalion's Invictus Company. *'We always hear about how many people died during the war ... [when you] see the endless rows of headstones, that number takes on a much greater significance.'*

AUTUMN 2022

›› Antigua adventures

A group of cadets from Cumbria ACF took part in the inaugural visit of a UK Cadet Force to Antigua in October. The group of 13 cadets and four CFAVs were hosted by the Antigua and Barbuda Defence Force (ABDF) during the 12-day trip.

Highlights of the life-changing adventure included cadets spending a day aboard UK patrol warship HMS Medway, taking part in the country's Independence Day parade, dinghy sailing and meeting the Governor-General of Antigua and Barbuda, the Resident British Commissioner and Chief of Defence Staff.

Two cadets from ABDF joined Cumbria ACF's Easter Camp in 2023, and Cumbria ACF will return to Antigua in 2024 as part of a formal cadet exchange programme.

To Inspire To Achieve

›› Adventurous training in Cyprus

Shropshire ACF delivered an action-packed AT exercise in Cyprus for 24 cadets in October. Activities included mountain biking in the Troodos Mountains, and paddleboarding and kayaking in the Mediterranean. The most popular activity of the week, however, was scuba diving: cadets completed a 30-minute dive in a fish reserve on the Akrotiri Peninsula. They also visited several cultural hot spots and ancient sites to learn about Cyprus' history.

›› Cadets gained exciting new Fire and Rescue skills

Cadets from Buckinghamshire ACF's 4th Platoon in Aylesbury learnt some exciting new skills thanks to a new partnership with Buckinghamshire Fire & Rescue Service. Cadets took part in a pilot scheme throughout 2022, enrolling on a three-phase training programme and attending evening sessions to gain knowledge and experience of hose running, pumping, trauma care and casualty evacuation.

Five cadets were even invited to assist with activities at Aylesbury Fire Station's annual open day. Well done for the leadership and initiative shown by **LCpl Harry Isom**, **LCpl Haris Hussain**, **LCpl Jack McCormack**, **LCpl Hadley Noonan** and **LCpl Alex Graham**. Particular mention goes to **LCpl Harry Isom** who led a rescue demonstration in front of a big crowd.

» Opportunity to hone new leadership skills

An action-packed autumn event inspiring teenagers to 'be all they can be' was co-hosted by Alleyn's School CCF in London. The school partnered with YOU London to offer 11 uniformed youth groups the opportunity to get hands-on experience of leadership.

The two-day development weekend, aimed at young people between the ages of 15 and 18, featured practical challenges, theoretical discussion, and inspiring speakers from military, industry and emergency services backgrounds.

Major Benest, Alleyn's CCF Contingent Commander, said: *'The opportunities to offer hands-on leadership experience, coupled with inspirational talks, is vital to inspire and upskill the next generation. I am extremely proud of the staff, cadets and the wider Alleyn's team for making the weekend possible.'*

Challenges were run by the Met Police, Fire Brigade, St John Ambulance, Army, Royal Air Force, Royal Navy, Alleyn's CCF and Rheinmetall BAE Systems Land, and included hose work and engine drills, first aid triage, a gun run, collaborative flight simulation, STEM-based command tasks, a virtual-reality battle drill, an RC Challenger 2 tank assault course and the execution of a search warrant.

Speakers included Lib Peck (Director of the Mayor of London's newly established Violence Reduction Unit), the Lord-Lieutenant of Greater London Sir Kenneth Olisa OBE, endurance athlete Major (retd) Sally Orange and Chris Grant, chair of both the British Basketball Federation and English Football's Integrated Coaching Board.

» Cadets took part in moving tributes during Belgium trip

In October, Oxfordshire ACF sent 55 cadets and CFAVs to Belgium on the Eurostar. The trip included the laying of a wreath to the fallen at the Royal Engineers grave at Railway Wood. Cadets also learnt about the Battle of Passchendaele at the Memorial Museum Passchendaele 1917 and visited the site where it took place. A highlight was when cadets joined the parade to the Menin Gate with the Last Post Association (pictured above).

AUTUMN

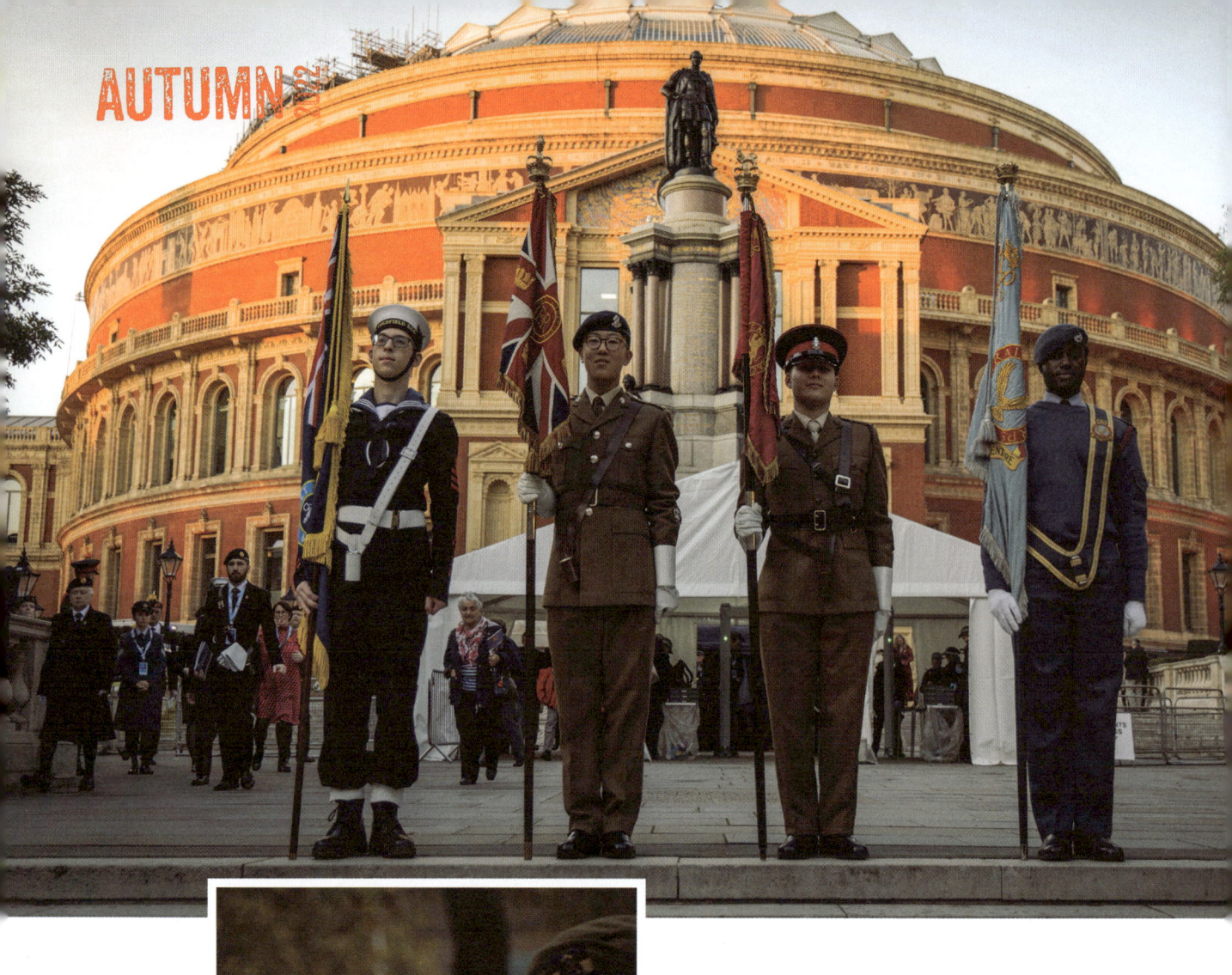

›› Remembrance parades

Cadets and adults from every detachment were out in force on the weekend of 11-13 November to take leading roles in Remembrance services, commemorations and parades. Cadets across the country laid wreaths, led parades and took part in ceremonies to help ensure that those who gave their lives for our country are never forgotten.

Pictured are a selection of cadets and CFAVs from Hampshire and Isle of Wight ACF and Newcastle Royal Grammar School CCF who were chosen to represent the Army Cadets nationally. They made the journey to the Royal Albert Hall for the Festival of Remembrance on Saturday 12 November along with a march past the Cenotaph in Whitehall on the Sunday.

YEAR IN FOCUS

Photos: Kate Knight and Mitchell Allen

Army Cadet Yearbook Issue 4

WINTER 2022/3

» Triumphant return of Rorke's Drift Concert

Musicians of Gwent and Powys ACF were joined by others from across the UK in the annual Rorke's Drift Concert at Brecon's Theatr Brycheiniog in February. It was the 23rd time the event had taken place and was a triumphant return after being put on hold for a few years due to adverse weather and the pandemic.

» New Year Honours success

Two members of the Army Cadets family received MBEs in the King's New Year Honours List 2023.

Army Cadets National Ambassador Jordan Wylie (top right) received an MBE for his outstanding contribution to charity and children's education on the Horn of Africa. Major Derek Munro (right) was honoured for his exceptional work as Cadet Executive Officer of Brent and Powys ACF. Huge congratulations to both!

» Cadets made life-saving snow rescue

In December, cadets **Brandon**, **Sam** (both 15) and **Toby** (16) of Tunbridge Wells Detachment, Kent ACF, were mentioned on the BBC News website for going to the aid of motorists stranded in the snow. Their involvement included helping a young couple with a four-week-old baby push their car to the top of a hill. ACCT UK invited a Praiseworthy Action nomination.

» Special recognition from ACCT UK

Pl Nadine Howard (Bedfordshire and Hertfordshire ACF) achieved the rare and very prestigious Meritorious Action Certificate (the higher of the two ACCT UK awards). In December, Nadine witnessed a car crash and immediately went to help. A 50-year-old female victim was lapsing in and out of consciousness and complained of severe back and neck pain. Leaving her own two young children with a bystander, Nadine climbed into the back of the woman's car to support her head and safeguard her neck and back. After 30 minutes the police arrived and asked Nadine to maintain support while they took over managing her children until an ambulance arrived 45 minutes later. She continued to assist while paramedics looked after the casualty.

Furthermore, after nomination by ACCT UK, Royal Humane Society (RHS) Awards Resuscitation Certificates were granted to **Lt Christopher Cooper**, **Squadron Leader Jonathan Evans**, **Maj Philip Anthony Hurley**, **Capt Franco Rizzo**, **Emma Lambert** and **SSI Austin Snelson**. Three lives were saved by their successful resuscitation attempts.

» A royal welcome

Cadets and staff from Bolton Detachment (Royal Artillery) Anzio Company were proud to form part of a welcome party for HM King Charles III and Queen Camilla when they visited Bolton in January to mark the 150th anniversary of Bolton Town Hall. The cadets were hugely excited, especially **LCpl Nathan Jackson** and **LCpl James Flint** who had the privilege of shaking His Majesty's hand. The King thanked the young people who lined the steps of the Town Hall.

WINTER 2022/3

›› Skiing adventure in Bavaria

A group of 20 cadets and nine CFAVs was deployed to the Bavarian Alps for the epic Ex SKI CADET 2 trip in February. The Cadet Centre for Adventurous Training (CCAT) ran Basic Ski Alpine and Intermediate Ski Alpine courses throughout the week, accredited by Snowsport Scotland, which resulted in the group skiing at a different venue every day.

Photos: Mitch-Allen

32 To Inspire To Achieve

YEAR IN FOCUS

» Polar Preet broke world record

British Army Officer Preet Chandi broke two world records after a 922-mile (1,485km) trek across the Antarctic. It was the longest solo and unsupported polar ski expedition by a woman and set a new overall record. She trekked from the Hercules Inlet to the Reedy Glacier in 70 days and 16 hours. The previous world record of 907 miles (1,459.8km) had been set in 2015 by Lt Col (retd) Henry Worsley. Congratulations Preet!

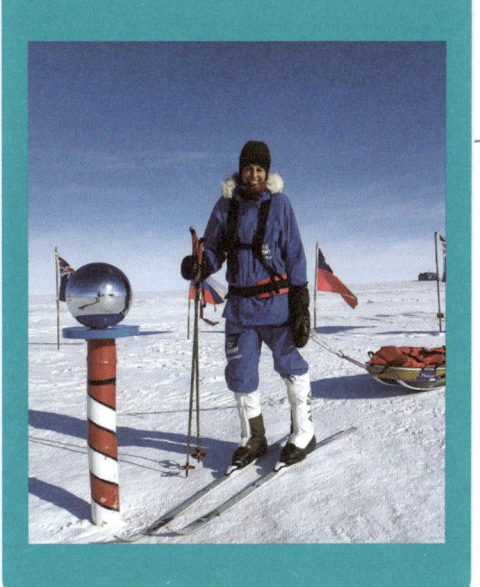

» Cadets' trip to India

The Army Cadets was delighted to be invited by India's National Cadet Corps (NCC), for the second year running, to take part in its India Youth Exchange Programme (YEP) in New Delhi.

Ten UK cadets from the Counties of Northumbria, Cambridgeshire, Leicestershire, Northamptonshire and Rutland, Oxfordshire, London SE, Gwent and Powys, and Suffolk went on the amazing 15-day trip, setting off from Heathrow on 11 January.

Cdt Sgt Rebecca Scott, **Cdt CSM Uashar Badakhshan**, **Cdt Sgt Kate Bilclough**, **Cdt RSM Thomas Dyer**, **Cdt SSgt Dominic Smith**, **Cdt CSM Oliver Wade**, **Cdt CSM Sasha Louwman**, **Cdt SSgt Rosie Walters**, **Cdt Sgt Abbie Addiscot Allen** and **Cdt Sgt Kevin Fresneda Jara** were accompanied by adult volunteers Lt Col Mike White (Northumbria ACF) and Capt Fiona Short (Greater Manchester ACF).

The packed itinerary included cultural, tourist and military visits, formal dinners, VIP receptions and parades. There was also an opportunity to meet India's Prime Minister, Shri Narendra Modi, and Defence Secretary Shri Giridhar Aramane I.A.S., plus an afternoon tea with President Smt Droupadi Murmu. NCC's motto is 'unity and discipline' and it has an incredible 1.2 million cadets across India.

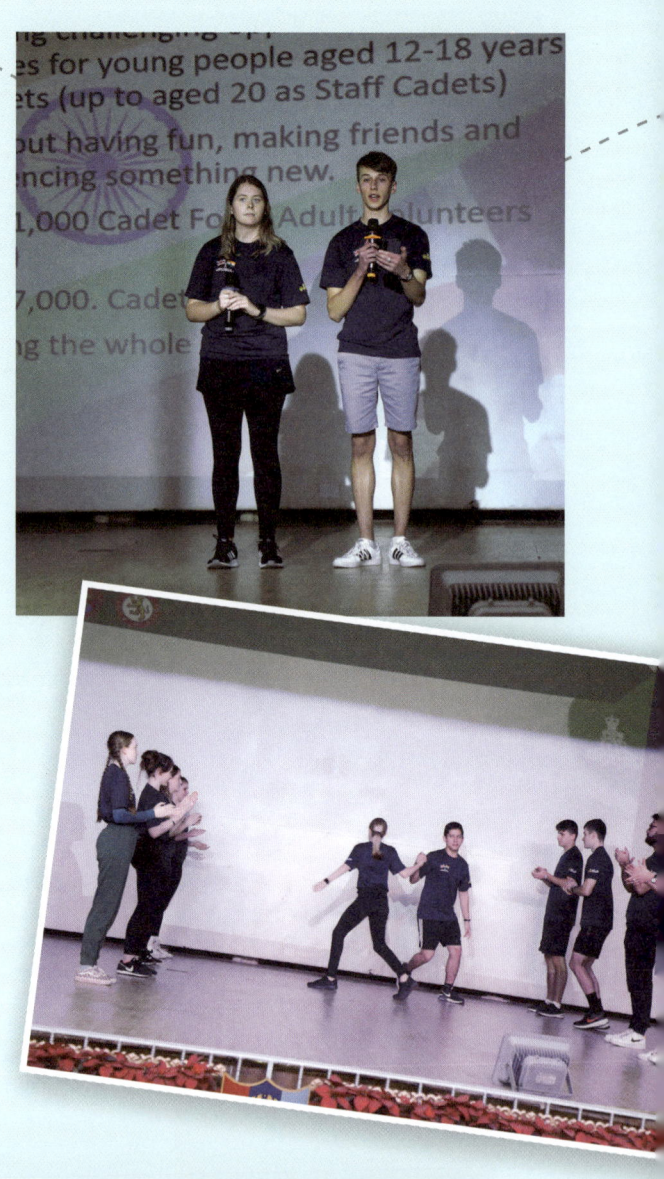

Cultural presentation

» Diary excerpts

The group kept a diary in which they recorded all of the brilliant activities they were invited to take part in. Here are a couple of excerpts:

'We listened to a presentation about Puneet Sagar Abhiyan – a fantastic climate change initiative which the NCC cadets have driven.'

'Indian food was always going to be a feature of our visit and we were introduced to thali – a platter made up of several different dishes to create a perfectly balanced meal. It was a little spicy for most but thoroughly enjoyable.'

In return, the UK hosted approximately 20 Indian cadets and adults in August 2023.

Clockwise from top: High tea at the home of NCC Director General Lt General Gurbirpal Singh; Defence Minister Hon Raksha Mantri's dinner event; India Gate visit

WINTER 2022/3

›› Highlights of the India trip

• Cultural presentations at HQ NCC from regions of India such as Gujarat, Punjab and Kerala

• A visit to the National War Memorial, National Museum and India Gate

• Dining at local restaurants

• Visits to the President and Prime Minister's homes

• Formal dinner hosted by the Defence Minister of India, Hon Raksha Mantri

• Visits to markets and malls

• Introduction to yoga at the Morarji Desai Institute of Yoga

• Attendance at the Independence Day celebrations at India Gate

• Inclusion in the PM Rally

• Visit to the Taj Mahal (one of the Seven Wonders of the World) and Agra Fort (UNESCO World Heritage Site)

• Each participating nation delivered a five-minute presentation on their country and a five-minute cultural dance. The UK contingent performed a traditional Scottish folk dance called Strip the Willow.

Top to bottom: Strip the Willow dance at the cultural presentation; Agra Fort visit; Introduction to yoga

YEAR IN FOCUS

❯❯ Making friends around the world

Friends were made from across the globe, with 19 international delegations involved in the programme: Seychelles, Russia, USA, UK, New Zealand, Kazakhstan, Tajikistan, Kyrgyzstan, Uzbekistan, Nepal, Brazil, Argentina, Vietnam, Mongolia, Mozambique, Sudan, Mauritius, Fiji and Maldives.

Language proved no barrier to communication. Cadets learnt the phrase 'Vasudhaiva Kutumbakam' (the world is one family) and discovered new ways to understand one another. For example, the UK cadets shared most of their coach journeys with cadets from the USA and Mongolia, and it was only a matter of time before music and song overcame any international hurdles.

Top: After the cultural presentations

Above: Capt Fiona Short ACF and Lt Col Mike White ACF meet NCC Director General Lt Gen Gurbirpal Singh

» Cadets honed winter skills in Norway

With the help of ACCT UK, Berkshire ACF sent 25 cadets and eight CFAVs to Norway in February for its biennial exchange with the Norwegian Home Guard Youth. The tradition of exchange between the two youth organisations has remained strong for 31 years.

The life-changing trip saw cadets complete adventurous tasks in harsh climatic conditions. Activities incorporated all the elements of winter skills training, including military cross-country and downhill skiing, plus fieldcraft. There was also a military history and culture experience during a trip to Oscarsborg Fortress. The exchange will be reciprocated when Berkshire ACF take on hosting responsibilities in summer 2024.

'It was the best thing I have done in the Cadets. The challenge pushed me to my limits,' said **Cdt RSM Dan Wakelin** from 11Pl Arborfield, while **Cdt Cpl Mia Lambert** said: *'I made great friends and did things I never thought I would do; it was absolutely amazing.'*

Photo: John Shirras

National Football winners

Junior boys South East
Senior boys South West
Junior girls West Midlands
Senior girls Northern Ireland

National X Rugby 7s winners

Intermediate boys Eastern
Senior boys Scotland
Intermediate girls Wales
Senior girls North West

» Energy, fun and friendship at ACF National Sports Championships

This year's ACF National Sports Championships for Football and Rugby delivered two fantastic weekends of fun, friendship, action and adventure.

All ten regions attended the National ACF Football Championship (25-26 February) and nine regions from across the UK competed in the National ACF Rugby Championship in Altcar (1-2 April).

'It was great to see so many cadets taking part in team sports. The spirit of the competition was loud and energetic with brilliant game play!' said SO2 Sports & PD Terry Hayter.

Ask at your detachment how you can get involved in regional events with Army Cadets sports. Senior cadets can apply for the Community Sports Award Level 3 through their regional sports adviser.

Army Cadet Yearbook Issue 4

SPRING 2023

›› Making music at Easter Camp

Nearly 500 cadets and CFAVs gathered at Otterburn Camp in Northumberland for Easter National Music Camp 2023. The event gave cadets from across the UK the opportunity to develop their musical skills, progress through star levels and take part in performances.

Camp members were joined by the Band of the Royal Regiment of Scotland, SO2 Training Richard Smith from Regional Command, Colonel Ashley Fulford (ACF Colonel Cadets) and National RSM David Lightfoot who enjoyed his first lesson on drum and triangle. Cadets and volunteers connected with each other as much as with the music: *'Attending national music camps has allowed me to meet like-minded people and make friendships with cadets from all over the country,'* said **Cdt Sgt Corey Kohut**, Cadet Force Music National Band Sgt Maj, Derbyshire ACF.

All cadets and CFAVs are welcome at National Music Camps, regardless of experience. If you are interested in learning a musical instrument, contact your detachment commander.

Cdt Drum Maj Newbury from Warwickshire with Lord Lingfield at Easter National Music Camp 2023

›› Stowe CCF biennial review

Stowe CCF underwent a successful biennial inspection which saw Army Section senior cadets take part in a number of activities, including a blank firing task and diving and rescuing a downed pilot. Army Section junior cadets took part in a round robin of stands, including Cadet GP 5.56mm rifle lessons and firing their first 5 round 'group and zero' shoot.

The inspecting officer was Colonel Edward Spinelli, Commander of 422nd Air Base Group, headquartered at RAF Croughton. He was joined by Countess Howe, His Majesty's Lord-Lieutenant of Buckinghamshire, hosted by Cdt FSgt Max James.

Colonel Spinelli remarked on the positive attitude, confidence, energy and achievements of the 200 Stowe cadets. The Lord-Lieutenant also commented how *'wonderful it was to be part of such a hive of activity, seeing all the sections going through their paces and clearly really enjoying themselves'*.

40   To Inspire To Achieve

ARMY CADETS COUNTY GRANT

YEAR IN FOCUS

» A thrilling jump from 3,500 feet

There was an exhilarating opportunity for nine cadets and four adult volunteers from 2nd (NI) Bn ACF to take part in a static-line parachute course and 3,500 feet jump at Netheravon. The five-day course in April included training carried out by the Army Parachute Team and a chance to meet the Red Devils parachute display team. The adrenaline-fuelled event counted as 4-Star AT of the cadet syllabus.

'I was filled with such joy and a sense of achievement as I had completed something amazing, potentially a once-in-a-lifetime opportunity,' said **Cdt Sgt Charley Hamilton**. *'I am forever grateful for the opportunities I have been given and continue to receive from the ACF, and I hope many more cadets get this opportunity too someday.'*

» Gina's big challenge for ACCT UK

Gina Allsop, Sports Officer and Adventure Training Officer for Sussex ACF, completed her biggest challenge to date in May with an epic unsupported mission.

Gina started her solo adventure by heading to Glasgow and joining the Kilt Walk. She then trekked the West Highland Way, before jumping in a boat at Fort William and paddling the Great Glen to Inverness (thanks to 51 Bde for storing her kayak). From there, she cycled back to Fort William. Throughout this amazing challenge she wild camped and carried all her food, raising money for ACCT UK, SSAFA and Sporting Force in the process.

SPRING 2022

›› Lord-Lieutenant's Cadets appointed

Lord-Lieutenants across the UK act as the King's personal representatives, and each appoints cadets annually to assist in official duties and events (such as accompanying the Lord-Lieutenant at high-profile civic and military occasions like Armed Forces Day, Remembrance Day and royal visits, or acting as an ambassador for their unit and the Army Cadets as an organisation). It is both a privilege and an honour to take on the role, which is typically given to those who have demonstrated outstanding service to their unit and the organisation. Nominations are made by their units' senior figures.

Cadets who received this prestigious title in spring 2023:

SCdt CSM Emma Ellison, 1st (NI) Bn ACF
Cdt RSM Scott Connor, Glasgow & Lanarkshire Bn ACF
Cdt CSM Keira Day, Cleveland ACF
Cdt Sgt Matthew Hunter, 1st (NI) Bn ACF
Cdt SSgt Hailee Rea-Crossley, Humberside & South Yorkshire ACF
Cdt SSgt Emily Burton, Cleveland ACF
Cdt Sgt Piper Noble, Humberside & South Yorkshire ACF
Cdt Cpl Darcey Woodman, 1st Bn The Highlanders ACF
Cdt CSM Jonty Jones, CCF – HQ South West
Cdt CSM Evan Morgan, Devon ACF
Cdt SM Jack Bishop, Norfolk ACF
Cdt Cpl Esme Richards, 1st Bn The Highlanders ACF
Cdt Cpl Andrew Taylor, Leicestershire, Northamptonshire & Rutland ACF
Cdt RSM Henry Turnbull, CCF – 4 Inf Bde and HQ NE
SCdt SM Andrew Savory, Devon ACF
Cdt CSM Philippa Tubridy, Leicestershire, Northamptonshire & Rutland ACF
SCdt SSgt Rebecca Scott, Northumbria ACF
SCdt SSgt Eleanor Hendricks, Wiltshire ACF
Cdt Cpl Ruby McCloy, 1st (NI) Bn ACF
Cdt Sgt Jack Bryson, 1st Bn The Highlanders ACF
Cdt Cpl Keanu Jones, 1st Bn The Highlanders ACF
Cdt SSgt Jessica Goodwin, Cleveland ACF
SCdt CSM Alfie Doherty, Warwickshire & West Midlands South Sector ACF
SCdt RSM Joshua Boundy, Sussex ACF
SCdt SSgt Nadia Cavanagh, Wiltshire ACF
SCdt Sgt Robert Allen, 1st (NI) Bn ACF
SCdt SSgt Leah Russell, Black Watch Bn ACF
SCdt CSM Chloe Bezer, Bedfordshire & Hertfordshire ACF
SCdt CSM Christopher Hunter, 1st (NI) Bn ACF
Cdt CSM Kacey Day, Cleveland ACF
Cdt Sgt Sarah Kane, 1st (NI) Bn ACF
Cdt Sgt Trinity Scanlon, 1st (NI) Bn ACF
Cdt Sgt Amelie Carbonell, Staffordshire & West Midlands North Sector ACF
Cdt SSgt Arlo Tait, Glasgow & Lanarkshire BN ACF
Cdt SSgt Daniel Quinn, Dorset ACF
Cdt SSgt Benjamin Woodcock, CCF – HQ Centre (East)
Cdt SSgt Oliver Hathaway-Smith, CCF – 11 Inf Bde & HQ SE
Cdt CSM Kai Greig, 1st Bn The Highlanders ACF
Cdt CSM Ben Marshall, Glasgow & Lanarkshire Bn ACF
Cdt RSM Lily Miller, Bedfordshire & Hertfordshire ACF
Cdt CSM Evelyn Robbie, Buckinghamshire (The Rifles) ACF
Cdt RSM Calan McGerty, West Lowland Bn ACF
Cdt Sgt Robert Turkington, CCF – 38 Irish Bde
Cdt Cpl Simrun Dhugga, Leicestershire, Northamptonshire & Rutland ACF
Cdt Sgt Jake Burnside, Lothian & Borders Bn ACF
Cdt RSM Georgina Lees, CCF – 11 Inf Bde & HQ SE
Cdt Sgt Danni Crehan, 1st Bn The Highlanders ACF
Cdt LCpl Callum Rawlings, West Lowland Bn ACF
Cdt Sgt Sylvan Tarn, CCF – 4 Inf Bde & HQ NE
Cdt Cpl Abigail Hardy, Staffordshire & West Midlands North Sector ACF
Cdt CSM Sophie Dmytrowich, Cleveland ACF
Cdt Cpl Callum Sutherland, 1st Bn The Highlanders ACF
Cdt Sgt Kaitlyn Beggs, 1st (NI) Bn ACF
Cdt Cpl Grace Thompson, 1st (NI) Bn ACF
SCdt Sgt Jorja Wilson, 1st (NI) Bn ACF
Cdt Sgt Owen Brumby, CCF – 160 Inf Bde & HQ Wales
SCdt CSM Thomas Burns, Lancashire ACF
Cdt Cpl Faith Steen, 1st (NI) Bn ACF
Cdt SSgt Nicole Hughes, CCF – 38 Irish Bde
SCdt SM Jack Shorey, Essex ACF
SCdt SM Fay Giles, Wiltshire ACF
Cdt SSgt Kieran Elsey, Lincolnshire ACF
Cdt Sgt Callum Prideaux, 1st Bn The Highlanders ACF
SCdt CSM Charlotte Trewick, Leicestershire, Northamptonshire & Rutland ACF
SCdt Sgt Dale Clendinning, 1st (NI) Bn ACF
CCpl Kerri Paton, CCF – 51 Inf Bde & HQ Scotland
Cdt Cpl India Massa, Derbyshire ACF (Mercian Regiment)
Cdt Sgt Naomi Bennett, CCF – 38 Irish Bde

SPRING 2022

❯❯ Hele's School celebrates 80 years of cadet activity

In May, staff, cadets and guests (among them former contingent commanders, whose appointments date back to the 1970s) celebrated 80 years of cadet activity at Hele's School CCF in Plymouth. The event showcased all that has been achieved in the unit over that time, as well as current developments and opportunities.

A lunch and presentation about the history of cadet activity at the school were followed by messages from former cadets about how their experiences have helped them in their career paths. Guests then witnessed cadets undergoing skill at arms training, learning first aid and shooting on the school's 24m indoor range.

Former commanders handed out a number of promotions, including one for the school's head girl and CCF **Cdt Grace Weaver**, who became Cadet Company Sergeant Major for the Army Section. Grace was presented with the Pete Stabb Pace Stick, kindly donated by a former master cadet. The General Monck Coldstream Guards Award, presented by former contingent commander Tony Williams MBE, was given to **Cdt Lily Dyson**.

❯❯ Cadet success at Ten Tors

Army Cadets teams from the counties of Cornwall, Devon, Dorset, Gloucestershire, Somerset and Wiltshire took part in the annual Ten Tors Challenge in April.

CFAVs and cadets spent seven months training and organising themselves for the two-day event, which saw teams navigate routes of 35, 45 or 55 miles across Dartmoor, visiting ten tors (or checkpoints) along the way. They carried all they needed to stay overnight and complete the route. Terrain, distances and the weather all presented challenges, so commitment, training, endurance and grit were vital.

A huge well done to all teams that took part in the challenge. If you are in the South West region and are interested in taking part in Ten Tors, speak to your detachment commander.

To Inspire To Achieve

» Coronation Champion

In partnership with Her Majesty Queen Camilla, the Royal Voluntary Service launched the Coronation Champions Awards for volunteers who have demonstrated exceptional dedication and significantly contributed to their community.

Among the 500 winners was **Cdt Sgt Emily Allen** of Humberside & South Yorkshire ACF. She received an official Coronation Champions pin, a certificate signed from both Their Majesties and two tickets to the Coronation Concert. Emily completed a Care Home Initiative during the Covid-19 pandemic, where she organised the writing of 293 letters to residents and the delivery of staff care packages to seven local care homes. She is also a dedicated fundraiser for charities including SSAFA, Walking With The Wounded and Royal British Legion, and mentors a boy with autism.

Emily said: *'I feel truly honoured. What I did and continue to do isn't for recognition, award or praise. By supporting each other, we can strengthen our community.'*

Emily with her mentee

Congratulations to Emily and the other Army Cadet Force nominees:

SI Pipemajor Lorna Angus, Glasgow & Lanarkshire ACF
Capt Anthony Ellison, Greater London South East Sector ACF
Maj Judy Sutherland, Greater London South East Sector ACF
SSI Andrew Wixon, Greater London South East Sector ACF
SSI Amanda Wixon, Greater London South East Sector ACF
RSMI Peter Harrison, Greater London South East Sector ACF
SMI John Johnstone, 1st (NI) Bn ACF
Cdt William Smith, 2nd (NI) Bn ACF
Capt James Douet, Surrey ACF
SI Trinity Muller, Surrey ACF
2Lt Stephen Hoydan, Bristol ACF

» Walking for veterans

March in March, a ten-mile walking challenge in aid of Combat Stress, saw 67 individual cadets and nine regional teams take great strides for charity. All money raised went towards the life-saving treatment the charity provides for veterans with severe mental health issues. At the time of publishing, the teams had raised over £4,800. Well done to everyone involved.

SPRING 2022

Photo: Crown Copyright Army Cadets UK

» Ex TELEMARK CHALLENGER

An epic 14-day skiing expedition in Norway in May was an awesome adventure for 16 cadets from across the UK.

The immense Ex TELEMARK CHALLENGER, supported by The Ulysses Trust, retraced the route taken by the Telemark saboteurs in the Second World War (this group of heroic resistance fighters risked their lives to sabotage a Nazi nuclear programme, altering the course of the war). Phase one involved a six-day Nordic ski touring training package, while phase two saw the group embark on a five-day self-sufficient ski tour across Hardangervidda (northern Europe's highest mountain plateau), utilising pulks (sleds) and dog-sleigh teams.

The AT expedition was a physical and mental challenge in sub-zero temperatures, but it was also an incredible opportunity for personal development and building self-confidence. *'I've learnt more than I could ever imagine! Thanks to everyone for the opportunity of a lifetime,'* said participant **Cdt Cpl Ellis**.

To Inspire To Achieve

» Cadets from Antigua visit Cumbria ACF

Cumbria ACF played host to cadets from Antigua and Barbuda for a week in April, following a successful trip to Antigua in October 2022 as part of an exchange programme between the cadet forces.

Cadets enjoyed a jam-packed programme of activities that displayed British life in all its diversity. They participated in the Lake District Sheep Dog Experience, took a lake cruise to Ambleside, participated in STEM activities at Barrow detachment, gained historical knowledge with museum and castle trips, visited an indoor shooting range, and completed fieldcraft and drill exercises.

A final parade concluded their time together, including a presentation and a number of cadets being awarded star-level passes.

Scan the QR code to watch footage of the exchange.

» CFAVs at Sandhurst

CFAVs from across the UK returned for the first face-to-face Initial Officer Training Course at Royal Military Academy Sandhurst (RMAS) since before the pandemic (when it was delivered virtually, then subsequently at Altcar Training Camp).

In May, 60 CFAVs who had been selected for commission at the Army Cadet Commissions Board in Wiltshire attended two modules at the Royal Military Academy: Development (which focused on introduction to leadership) and Confirmatory (which put the theory into practice). On completion of both modules (and after two years of time served and 20 days of cadet activity), CFAVs became eligible for promotion to Lieutenant.

'This course was one of the best I have been on in my Cadets service,' said 2Lt Andy Mead ACF. *'I enjoyed every minute and would recommend it to everybody.'*

SUMMER 2023

» Fun-filled display at Royal Cornwall Show

Cadets from Cornwall ACF demonstrated the value of Army Cadets to the public with a professional and engaging display at this year's Royal Cornwall Show. An observation trail (where children were asked to look for a cadet's lost equipment) and new paintball target range proved particularly popular – local radio personalities from Pirate FM even took part in the paintballing! A special shout-out to **Cdt LCpl Crouchman** from Launceston detachment who dressed in a ghillie suit and came third in the Pirate FM mascot dance-off.

Army Cadets National Ambassador Jordan Wylie (left) supported the fundraising efforts by jogging four miles and spending time with cadets and CCF staff

» Smile4Wessex

Cadets and CFAVs from Thomas Hardye School CCF in Dorchester took part in the 2x2x24 Challenge: walking, jogging or running two miles, every two hours, over a 24-hour period.

They raised money for Smile4Wessex, which funds cutting-edge medical equipment and treatments for the Wessex Neurological Centre in Southampton. The link with the charity was made after a CFAV became critically ill following a cadet training weekend and was taken to Wessex Neurological Centre for life-saving emergency surgeries.

To Inspire To Achieve

›› International Cadet Cup

In May, the third International Cadet Cup took place in Hungary. **Cdt Cpl Claudiu Leonard Doroftei**, **Cdt Sgt Harvey Elliott**, **Cdt Myles Mason** (all Bristol ACF) and **Cdt LCpl Eleanor Curnow** (Cornwall ACF) were accompanied by Maj Dennis Hull and Lt Poppy Gates to the under-18s athletic event, which is run by the Hungarian Ministry of Defence.

Cadets took part in a number of events which were run and supervised by the Hungarian Army, including laser run shooting, a labyrinth matrix run, first aid, hand grenade throwing, distance estimation, an obstacle course and a relay run with rifle. The competition culminated in a prize-giving presentation.

Maj Hull said: *'The event pushed the cadets to their limits physically and mentally, but they thoroughly enjoyed it!'*

›› Poignant battlefield tours

Two Counties got to witness the impact war can have on landscapes and lives during battlefield tours. Both excursions were made possible due to grants from ACCT UK and were an opportunity to pay respects to those who made the ultimate sacrifice for their country.

More than 30 cadets from Norfolk ACF's Artillery Battery, Engineer Squadron and Britannia Company attended a five-day WW2 battlefield tour of Dunkirk. The group followed the route taken by the 2nd Battalion Royal Norfolk Regiment during the campaign. A solemn but important highlight was a visit to pay respects to the 97 Royal Norfolk POWs who died at the hands of the SS at Le Paradis.

A group of 86 cadets and 14 CFAVs from Dyfed and Glamorgan ACF visited Ypres in Belgium for the two-day battlefield study Ex DREIGIAU CADLANC.

They visited cemeteries, museums and First World War trenches in Sanctuary Wood and Hooge Crater. A particularly moving moment was a wreath laying at the Welsh cromlech (pictured) at Pilckem Ridge, where an imposing Welsh dragon memorialises those of Welsh descent who took part in the First World War. Dyfed and Glamorgan ACF raised £10,000 for it to be built and were one of its highest fundraisers.

Cadets also took centre stage at the Menin Gate Last Post Ceremony alongside the Military Wives Choir. *'They were watched by hundreds of members of the public and did the ACF proud,'* said Maj Richard Holder, Assistant Commandant, Dyfed and Glamorgan ACF. *'I also had the honour of reciting the exhortation before the minute's silence.'*

SUMMER 2023

» Musical spectacle

The ACCT Scotland Beating Retreat made a triumphant return after a four-year break. Cadets from across the UK came together to perform at Edinburgh Castle for the musical extravaganza.

It included a massed bands display, a light infantry bugling spectacle, and a massed Pipes and Drums display. There were over 130 Army Cadet musicians involved from Scotland, Durham ACF, Gwent and Powys ACF and Campbell College CCF, as well as guests from the Royal Air Force Air Cadets.

Col Ashley Fulford, National Colonel Cadets, said it was *'an outstanding event that made all of us who are associated with the Cadets very proud – well done to everyone involved'.*

Particular congratulations to **Cdt Bandmaster Tom Lord** who led the massed bands, **National Senior Drum Major Kayleigh Young** who led the Pipes and Drums, and **National Cdt Pipe Major Rowan Laws** who played the solo part in *Amazing Grace* (all Black Watch Bn ACF).

Photos: Dougie Johnston

YEAR IN FOCUS

» RideLondon

Congratulations to SSI Donna Hawley (adult instructor for Yorkshire North and West ACF), Rebecca Trinity Jones (former cadet) and Rob Warner (ACCT UK supporter through his employer Ammo & Co which runs Cadet Kit Shop) for conquering the 100-mile RideLondon cycling challenge.

Their efforts have raised £1,897.25 to support cadets and adult volunteers.

Inspired? Register your interest for RideLondon by emailing **fundraising@acctuk.org**

» Ex WAR HORSE

Thanks to generous grants from South East Reserve Forces' and Cadets' Association and The Connaught Trust, cadets from Hampshire and Isle of Wight ACF travelled to Flanders, Belgium, at Easter for Ex WAR HORSE – a special tour of the First World War battlefields of the Western Front.

The County's Dettingen Music Band led the trip (supported by band members from Derbyshire ACF and Gwent and Powys ACF), which incorporated visits to war cemeteries and culminated in a poignant drumhead service at Tyne Cot Commonwealth War Graves Cemetery, and a moving parade and performance at the Menin Gate.

'I am immensely proud of the hard work and dedication of our cadets and CFAVs who ... put on a string of great performances and acts of remembrance in and around Ypres,' said Col Tim Hope MBE, Commandant of Hampshire and Isle of Wight ACF.

CADETS & the CORONATION

King Charles III and Queen Camilla travelling in the 260-year-old Gold State Coach

The coronation of King Charles III took place at Westminster Abbey on Saturday 6 May. Representatives from Army Cadets had the once-in-a-lifetime privilege of being involved in the splendour and pageantry of the day.

Left: Cdt RSM Josh Watson (St Columba's College CCF)

Right: Staff Cdt RSM Joshua Siggers (Kent ACF)

Bearing banners with pride

Two army cadets had the honour of representing Army Cadets (both ACF and CCF) as banner bearers during the coronation pageantry. **Staff Cdt RSM Joshua Siggers** (Kent ACF) and **Cdt RSM Josh Watson** (St Columba's College CCF) led the Military Marching Band of the Duke of York's Royal Military School CCF and marched from MOD Main Building to Parliament Square. They then stood alongside 100 banner bearers of the Royal British Legion and watched as members of the armed forces escorted HM King Charles III to Westminster Abbey.

After the service in the Abbey, the banner bearers and musicians were able to watch the new King and Queen travelling in the 260-year-old Gold State Coach back to Buckingham Palace. They then marched over Westminster Bridge to continue in the coronation celebrations.

'It was an absolute honour to take part in the coronation of King Charles III and to be part of the amazing atmosphere in London,' said Staff Cdt RSM Joshua. *'To see the members of all the armed forces form up in front of us, and then to see the King go past in the Gold State Coach, made for an incredible experience.'*

Over 4,000 members of the UK's armed forces took part in what the Ministry of Defence has called the largest military ceremonial operation of its kind for a generation.

> 'To see the members of all the armed forces form up in front of us, and then see the King go past in the Gold State Coach, made for an incredible experience'

Members of the Cadet Forces bearing banners at CTC Frimley Park and taking part in the ceremony

Cadets and CFAVs representing Army Cadets in the stands at Admiralty Arch

Admiring from Admiralty Arch

It was a privilege for 65 cadets and CFAVs to represent Army Cadets during the formal celebration on coronation day. The cadets, who travelled from Bristol, Scotland, Surrey and the Highlands, were invited to be spectators in the stands at Admiralty Arch and to watch the pageantry up close.

The cadets and CFAVs were also some of the first to arrive at the gates to Buckingham Palace to witness the King and Queen's entrance onto the balcony and a flypast from the Royal Air Force.

Since the coronation of Edward VII in 1902, it has become customary for a newly crowned monarch to greet the crowds in The Mall from the Buckingham Palace balcony after the ceremony. King Charles and Queen Camilla continued the tradition and appeared with the royals who had taken part in the procession.

YEAR IN FOCUS

The Prince and Princess of Wales with Prince Louis wave at crowds during carriage procession

Cadets and CFAVs watched as members of the UK's armed forces took part in the largest military ceremonial operation of its kind for a generation

The Military Marching Band of The Duke of York's Royal Military School CCF

56

YEAR IN FOCUS

The Military Marching Band of The Duke of York's Royal Military School CCF during rehearsals for the coronation

'The band stepped up their usual rehearsals to prepare for their prestigious part'

Historic day for Dukies

Thirty-five members of The Duke of York's Royal Military School CCF were given the honour of playing at the coronation of King Charles III.

Dukies from the school's Military Marching Band, including **Drum Major Kieran Nasau**, **Band JUO Ben Thorne** and **Band CSM Charlotte Trimby**, performed throughout the coronation to entertain the crowds.

The band stepped up their usual rehearsals to prepare for their prestigious part within the coronation pageantry.

The musicians have previously had some amazing opportunities to play, such as at Twickenham Stadium for the England vs Argentina rugby game and the police passing-out parade in Hendon. However, the coronation of King Charles will definitely be one for the school's history books.

Cambridgeshire celebrations

Cambridgeshire ACF commemorated VE Day alongside coronation celebrations with a series of events on 7 and 8 May.

On Sunday, Chatteris cadets attended a church service to commemorate the coronation. Then, on Monday, they served afternoon tea to the community at the Royal British Legion's Chatteris branch.

Cadets at Ramsey and Newmarket took part in memorial services. At the latter, standard bearer **Cdt Sgt Miles** laid the standard and **Cdt D'Arcy** laid a wreath. Cadets then demonstrated activities such as first aid and fieldcraft at a recruitment stand at Newmarket Coronation Fair. Newmarket Detachment Commander SSI Drummond said: 'The cadets have done very well. We have had great comments from the RBL, and the Parade Marshall specifically praised Cdt Sgt Miles for her drills. We have had a great turnout and I'm really impressed with the effort the cadets have made and everything they have done today.'

Above: Cadets serve afternoon tea.
Left: Newmarket Coronation Fair recruitment stand

Coronation concert win for Cumbria cadets

Two lucky cadets from Cumbria ACF – **Cdt Cpl Jasmine Bell** from Longtown and **Cdt LCpl Ziva Scott** of Kendal – were among attendees of the Coronation Concert at Windsor Castle.

The concert tickets were generously donated by the former Lord-Lieutenant of Cumbria, Mrs Claire Hensman CVO, and were awarded as prizes by Cumbria ACF to the top cadet and most improved cadet in the skills of fieldcraft at their recent camp. Their commandant, Col Guy Harnby, recognised their success: 'Both Jasmine and Ziva thoroughly deserve the recognition they achieved among their peers at our recent fieldcraft camp and are role models for all our cadets in the County. I'm thrilled to hear how much they loved their prize and how much they enjoyed the concert in front of His Majesty The King and Her Majesty The Queen.'

Cdt Cpl Jasmine Bell and Cdt LCpl Ziva Scott at the Coronation Concert

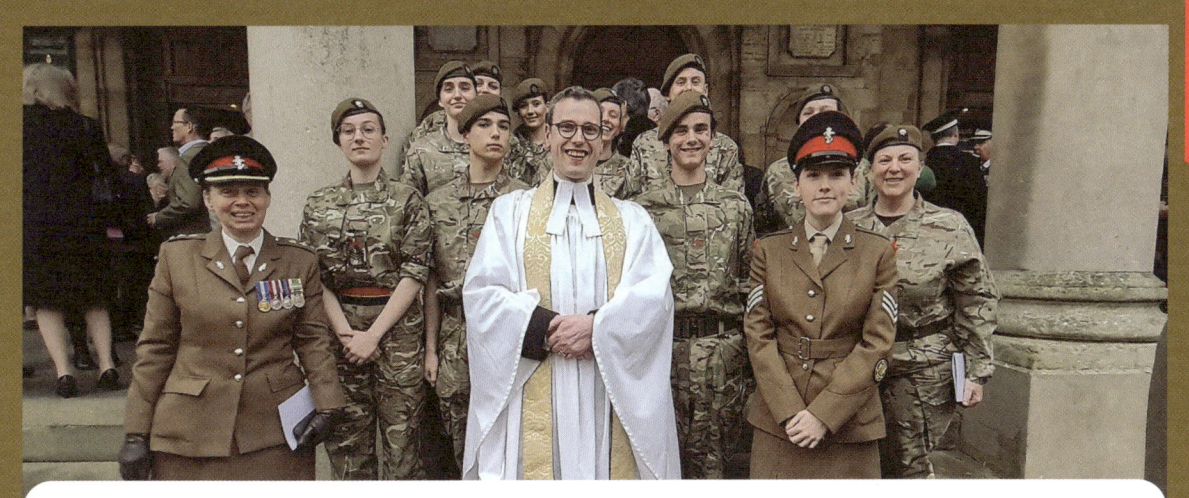

Northamptonshire and Rutland service

On 30 April, D Company (Leicestershire, Northamptonshire and Rutland ACF) were invited to attend Choral Evensong at All Saints' Church Northampton in the week of prayer leading up to the King's coronation.

Padre Major Oliver Coss led the mixed-faith congregation through prayer and worship to celebrate the coming coronation. The event was attended by Lord-Lieutenant of Northamptonshire Sir James Saunders Watson and other important dignitaries and honoured guests.

HM Lord-Lieutenant Sir James Saunders Watson said he was *'very grateful to have the support of such smart, professional and well-turned-out cadets in attendance'*.

All those who attended appreciated the opportunity to reflect on the Monarch's service in his previous position as the Prince of Wales, and looked forward to seeing his continuing support of different faiths as King of England.

Wiltshire CFAV families day

Wiltshire ACF hosted a CFAV families day on Sunday 7 May. The event, which was held in conjunction with coronation celebrations, gave Commandant Colonel Britt Haggerty a chance to show her appreciation to the CFAVs and their families.

There was a hog roast as well as bouncy castles, slides, games, raffles (in aid of ACCT UK), presentations – and glorious sunshine.

Murdo Urquhart, chief executive of ACCT UK, was in attendance and presented a certificate of appreciation to Col Haggerty.

It was also an opportunity to present awards to the following Wiltshire ACF CFAVs for their years of dedicated service:

John Le Feuvre MBE, outgoing Cadet Executive Officer (CEO) of Wiltshire ACF.

James Donaldson, who gave 30 years of volunteer service to Wiltshire ACF (including 15 years of Ten Tors volunteering).

SMI Colin Brown, presented with his Cadet Force Medal (CFM), awarded after 12 years of Voluntary Service to the Army Cadet Force.

SSI Neil Ashley, awarded the Commandant's Coin for his exhaustive work in maintaining the historical archives of Wiltshire ACF.

SMI Colin Brown awarded CFM by Col Haggerty

Celebrating CCF 75

75 1948 - 2023 Combined Cadet Force

The Combined Cadet Force celebrated its 75th anniversary on 1 April 2023. We delve into the archives to explore its fascinating history.

On 1 April, the CCF marked 75 years of equipping young people with new skills, improved teamwork, confidence and leadership.

It was the start of a whole raft of celebrations, (running from April 2023 to April 2024), to commemorate the military-themed youth organisation's 75-year history (see timeline, over).

» The CCF in 2023

Currently, there are CCF contingents in more than 500 secondary schools across the UK, offering young people a host of challenging, exciting, adventurous and educational activities.

The CCF is renowned for helping young people develop personal responsibility, leadership and self-discipline, but also offers an outstanding selection of extra-curricular activities.

Opportunities may range from climbing mountains, learning to sail and flying a plane to making an incredible new set of friends. There are also plenty of chances to gain recognised qualifications in disciplines such as first aid, and to take part in national programmes such as DofE.

Each CCF is an educational partnership between the participating school and the Ministry of Defence (MOD) and may include Royal Navy, Royal Marines, Army or Royal Air Force sections.

'MOD-sponsored cadets have been a key part of the enrichment experience in schools since its first iteration prior to 1948, as a junior division of the Officers' Training Corps in selected independent schools,' said Brigadier Anthony Lamb, MOD Head of Youth & Cadets, CCF Contingent Commander and Deputy Head (Co-curriculum) at Eastbourne College.

'Today the modern CCF is a vibrant, 21st-century uniformed youth movement which is helping to transform the lives of young people across the social spectrum.

'The value doesn't just come from the cadet experience itself. What is already being recognised is that, for some, the cadet experience also acts as a catalyst that helps them unlock their self-belief and improve their engagement and wider learning across other aspects of the curriculum too.'

Cambrian Cadet Patrol

YEAR IN FOCUS

CCF history in pictures

Field Marshal Bernard Law Montgomery (Monty) inspects at Repton School in June 1954

Eastbourne College cadets in 1958

Colston's School Cadets NCOs in March 1917

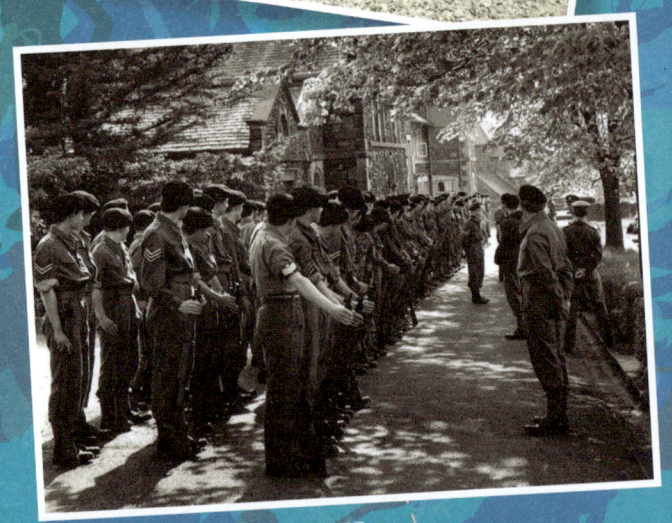

Sedbergh School cadet drill in 1967

CCF TIMELINE

» 1859

Forerunners of cadet forces in schools first appeared when a number of schools formed units for the defence of the UK in response to the threat of invasion by France. Although the threat receded, the units remained and, over time, more schools formed units which evolved into the Junior Officers' Training Corps, administered by the War Office.

» 1948

It was decided to combine all cadet units in schools into one organisation named the Combined Cadet Force (CCF), with contingents being able to have one or more service sections. There were 247 schools that accepted the invitation to adopt the new scheme and the new CCF was honoured by His Majesty King George VI becoming its Captain General.

» 1952

The Combined Cadet Force Association was established to represent all the schools with CCF units.

» 1953

Her Majesty Queen Elizabeth II became the Captain General of the CCF.

YEAR IN FOCUS

Sedbergh School guard inspection in 1987

Epsom College Cadets in 1906

Eastbourne College in 1952

Eastbourne College at Tidworth Pennings Camp in July 1922

» 2010

The cadet forces celebrated their 150th anniversary throughout 2010. On 7 July there was a Royal Review, when cadets and adult volunteers from all cadet forces marched down The Mall. King Charles III (then Prince of Wales) took the salute outside Clarence House, which was followed by a Royal Garden Party in Buckingham Palace.

» 2012

The government launched the Cadet Expansion Programme (CEP) to strengthen the cadet forces. The aim of the CEP was to form new cadet units in English state-funded secondary schools, focusing on state schools in areas of high deprivation. It was a joint MOD and Department for Education programme. £50 million from LIBOR fines was committed to the programme.

» 2023

Since the start of CEP in 2012, 362 schools have been approved to establish a cadet unit. The Government's ambition now is to increase the number of cadets in schools from 43,000 to 60,000 by April 2024. This has completely changed the shape of the CCF from being an organisation where independent school contingents outnumbered state school contingents, to now being one where state school contingents are in the majority.

❯❯ Royalty and the CCF

The CCF has a long and fascinating history, which includes royal patronage. In February 2010, Barnaby Spink (pictured right with Her Majesty Queen Elizabeth II) was one of just 26 cadets selected to meet the Monarch for the launch of the cadet movement's 150th anniversary.

The late Queen was the patron of Cadet 150, a programme of 150 events which took place across the cadet movement that year. At the time she was also Captain General of the CCF.

Former head boy Barnaby was nominated for the honour due to his outstanding commitment to the CCF: at the time he was the Lord-Lieutenant's Cadet for Cambridgeshire and a Cdt Sgt in Kimbolton School CCF.

'In came the Queen and Prince Philip and we spoke with them about all the cadet movement could offer young people'

'We had only received a loose itinerary for the weekend,' he said. *'We knew we would be seeing key sites, including the Ministry of Defence HQ and Buckingham Palace, but we had no idea who we would meet.*

'Beyond our wildest expectations, as we stood in the Bow Room of Buckingham Palace, in came the Queen and Prince Philip and for half an hour we spoke with them about all the cadet movement could offer young people.'

Delving even further back into the archives, the image top right shows His Majesty King George VI in his capacity as the Captain General of the CCF. He was inspecting part of the Signal Platoon of Portsmouth Grammar School CCF at Bourley Camp, Aldershot, on 9 August 1948.

To Inspire To Achieve

Go further

Scan the QR code to watch original British Pathé film footage of His Majesty King George VI inspecting cadets at Bourley Camp, Aldershot.

Photo: Portsmouth Grammar School Archive

65

ADVENTURERS

Meet some incredible adventurers. Discover what it's like to find yourself in extreme, exhilarating and sometimes terrifying environments, using your skills and training to complete your mission ...

Photo: Daniel Struthers

Ed walked the entire length (4,225 miles) of the Amazon River

AMAZON ADVEN

Photo: Keith Ducatel

Meet former cadet **Ed Stafford**, the first man to walk the entire length of the world's longest river.

Ed Stafford is the 21st-century embodiment of an adventure hero. He holds the Guinness World Record for being the first human to walk the entire length (4,225 miles) of the Amazon River, a journey that saw him held up at arrow point and mistakenly arrested for murder. The former soldier also spent two months alone on the Pacific island of Olorua for the Discovery Channel UK's *Naked and Marooned*.

To raise social awareness, he lived with travelling communities for Channel 4's *60 Days with the Gypsies* and experienced first-hand the hardships faced by residents on some of the UK's most troubled housing estates for Channel 4's *60 Days on the Estates*.

» Tell us about your time as a cadet

I went to Uppingham School in Rutland, and Cadets was one of the areas in which it excelled. Joining harnessed my energy that was being misplaced by being naughty and disruptive (I got into trouble for chopping down a tree the Queen had planted!). I was in the Royal Marine Cadets and made the rank of Sergeant. It enabled me to channel my passion for being outdoors into something practical, learning new skills such as weapon handling.

The whole camp experience had a real impact on me and made me want to join the military. I never wanted to sit behind a desk.

'A tribal chief was furious that my passport wasn't signed personally by the Queen'

Ed Stafford First Man Out available to stream now on discovery+

TURER

» In 2010 you walked the length of the Amazon – why?

I'd always had it in the back of my mind. The idea of going downriver, being the first to navigate it from source to sea, and interacting with indigenous communities appealed to me. I thought about how much more visually stimulating and incredible it would be to do it on foot, looking into the whites of the eyes of a tribal chief. It would draw upon soft skills – like humility – that enable people to trust you. I'd be using these skills to stay alive, rather than dodging arrows from a plastic kayak in the middle of the river.

I disagreed with those who said it would be impossible – it's walking from A to B, albeit 4,225 miles. But I didn't realise how hard it would be, especially when my 20-strong team wound up being just two: me and my guide Cho.

» What part of the adventure was most challenging?

I was naive and didn't understand how indigenous people might think. My piece of paper with permission to be there meant nothing to them: they couldn't read, and not many spoke Spanish.

I was held at gunpoint and arrow point; I lost count of the number of times I was told we would die. It made me nervous at first, but then I realised being scared used up all my energy. I just had to listen, smile and think: *'I'm doing this now. If we die, we die.'* Luckily, Cho would do all the talking – he was quick to laugh and disarm them.

» Which moments stand out?

I was wrongly arrested for murder, having turned up the day after a man had gone missing. I was detained overnight, with four people standing round the house with guns, until a police officer turned up the next morning and let me go. On another occasion, a tribal chief was furious that my passport wasn't signed personally by the Queen.

» How did you cope in difficult times?

I set myself little goals. If I met them, I would be able to sleep in my hammock. My daily objectives were very functional for a few months: *'Have you moved forward? Have you eaten?'* A goal might have been just washing all the jungle grime away at the end of the day.

If I did such an expedition again, it would be with more maturity and as a more relaxed, socially engaging experience but, back then, I was at the edge of my capabilities.

» How did you cope spending two months on the deserted island of Olorua?

It was about devising strategies. You need a toolkit of things to keep yourself in a good frame of mind. The same was true in the pandemic when many people struggled with isolation. Managing your mental health is a responsibility in life.

Ed survived as a modern-day Robinson Crusoe on Olorua, an uninhabited island of the Lau Archipelago

» What was it like filming *60 Days with the Gypsies* and *60 Days on the Estates*?

It's a challenge to win a community's trust so they will let you into their world, enabling you to tell their stories and open viewers' eyes to something they don't normally see. It's similar to the nuances of getting a tribal chief onside when he's got every desire to stick an arrow in your head – although on the estate, it was actually a gun down a dark alley. It's about being nice and being human. It was a privilege and a rewarding experience.

» What inspired your love of the great outdoors?

Growing up in the Leicestershire countryside in the 1970s, I'd roam the fields with a posse of mates from my village. I'd say goodbye to my mum in the morning and come back as it was getting dark. We'd play football, build bivouacs, dam streams, run around with guns made out of sticks and go on manhunts which could last multiple days, despite having to go home for tea each evening. I was always shy in my social interactions with adults and didn't have a huge amount of confidence. The outdoors was the opposite of that; I felt more comfortable in myself.

ADVENTURERS

'I lost count of the number of times I was told we would die'

Ed Stafford First Man Out available to stream now on discovery+

» What did you like about being in the Army?

I went to Sandhurst in 1998, made the rank of captain and was assigned to the Army Training Regiment in Lichfield to train Stage 1 recruits. I think it was the relationships I formed with the men I commanded that I enjoyed most. Sometimes they have more life experience than you, so you can't go in and start bossing them around – they'll tell you where to go. It's all about "soft" skills: managing people to get them to want to do things for you. Also, we were pushed really hard – some of the exercises were tougher than the Amazon. It's good to know you can push your limits.

'Being in the Cadets gave me the kind of education you can't get in a classroom'

» You now live in Costa Rica. What's that like?

It's great! There are pumas, ocelots and snakes, but I'm not worried. It's so healthy for our children to grow up here.

Before our move my wife asked: *'Am I going to be cleaning this kitchen for the next 40 years of my life?'* We had fallen into the daily grind of school runs and play dates. Our son Ran is nearly six, our twin daughters are three, and it struck us that we had a window of opportunity for an amazing family adventure. I'm lucky that I can do what I do from anywhere. Costa Rica is a safe country with a great environmental ethos, having had success in reforestation over the last 30 years. Everyone we told said: *'I wish I could do that.'* Guess what? You can!

» What do you owe to having been in the Cadets?

A lot. It's all part and parcel of what's made me who I am. It helped prepare me for the military world, with all its challenges and rewards. It's easy to be lazy and do the least work possible, but the more you put into life, the more you get out. Being in the Cadets gave me the kind of education you can't get in a classroom.

SURVIVAL
state of mind

Meet **Megan Hine**, a world expert in all aspects of remote wilderness expeditions and a consultant on some of the biggest adventure shows on TV – she's even kept Bear Grylls safe on set.

You could say survival expert Megan Hine has seen and done it all. She's been chased through the jungle by armed opium-farm guards, abseiled past bears, and used tampons to light fires while in the wild. Never one to shy away from perilous conditions, Megan has coped with everything from sweltering deserts and humid jungles to precarious mountains and rapid rivers.

» Cadet power

She credits her passion for adventure and the great outdoors to her time as a cadet at Malvern College – first as an RAF cadet and then a Royal Marine cadet.

'There was a test to see if girls would be suitable to join the Royal Marines and I was chosen to be part of the research. Consequently, I was lucky enough to take part in loads of adventurous training.'

Megan's parents were academics and it was assumed she would study and possibly join the armed forces, but being a cadet opened her eyes to a whole new world.

'I took advantage of all the opportunities that arose, from winter climbing in Scotland to white-water kayaking. It really made me fall in love with exploring my limits, nature and wild places.'

> **'It started as a way of escaping the pressures put on me as a child. I found freedom in the outdoors as there were no boundaries'**

ADVENTURERS

Megan on her way back from the Altai Mountains

» Freedom beyond boundaries

Through leading expeditions and bushcraft courses (as well as being a survival expert on TV shows such as *Man vs. Wild* and *Running Wild with Bear Grylls*), Megan has explored far reaches of the globe in pursuit of adventure. The desire to find out what's round the next corner has always been with her, even when she was at school.

'It started as a way of escaping the pressures that were put on me as a child. I found freedom in the outdoors as there were no boundaries.

'I was good at sport and participated in all kinds of events, but I always struggled with the concept that I was on a pitch with imaginary boundaries when behind them lay the horizon. I really couldn't understand why I was confined when what I really wanted to be doing was exploring the world.'

Photo Daniel Struthers

> 'No amount of top-of-the-range kit will help in a survival situation if you don't have the right mindset'

Top: Megan outside a Mongolian ger. Below right: Megan with a golden eagle while living with the nomadic Kazakh people

Photos: Daniel Struthers

» Building resilience

Surviving in the wild takes a great deal of resilience and Megan has overcome situations with horrendous weather, lack of food and encounters with predators. She puts her ability to cope in these conditions down to the practical and physical skills she has acquired over the years, along with her mindset. She first learnt the benefit of having a resilient state of mind as a cadet and believes no amount of top-of-the-range kit will help in a survival situation if you don't have the right mindset.

'In the Cadets there's an opportunity to build resilience, which is your ability to bounce back from hardship. The best way to do this is to expose yourself to lots of different challenges and then overcome those challenges by stepping out of your comfort zone.

'Resilience is built by participating in lots of adventurous activities, socialising with different people and taking part in sporting competitions.

'Also, being a cadet teaches you to work in a team. So much of modern-day life is about competition instead of teamwork but, if you look at our ancestral roots, connecting with others is a fundamental part of being human.'

» Leadership challenges

Megan's leadership skills have sharpened with each fresh challenge she has undertaken.

'Gaining experience is one of the key components to being a good leader, which is why I think the Cadets provides such brilliant opportunities to learn how to lead. You are constantly pushing yourself out of your comfort zone, taking on leadership tasks and working as a team. Only through experience will you learn to trust yourself and gain the confidence to make mistakes.'

ADVENTURERS

Sisters in survival

There have been plenty of daredevil women like Megan in the history of climbing and travelling but they are not as well known as their male counterparts. Here are some she mentions in her book *Mind of a Survivor*.

In the 1760s, **Jeanne Baret** became the first woman to circumnavigate the globe and did so disguised as a man on a ship in the French navy.

Lady Hester Stanhope was a pioneering archaeologist who, in the early 1800s, explored the Middle East while carrying a sword and riding a white stallion.

In 1871, **Lucy Wallace** became the first woman to climb the Matterhorn, apparently living on a diet of Champagne and sponge cake.

'It's often assumed that women of today are the first female adventurers but it's just not true,' says Megan. *'While men were writing books about their exploits, women were off having amazing adventures but not really sharing them with the world.'*

She suggests that emotions such as shame, guilt and embarrassment can often arise when people first step into a leadership role – whether that's leading fellow cadets, making decisions in a work setting or taking people into a survival situation.

'Those kind of emotions often come to the fore when you step up and put yourself in a vulnerable position. However, if you get used to those feelings when you are young it will help you conquer them as you go through life.'

» Clarity of purpose

As a seasoned expedition leader, Megan offers a bespoke service where she turns people's dream adventures into reality. She also gives people the chance to take part in unique experiences such as the expedition she ran to Mongolia in September 2023. This trip to one of the most remote places on Earth included riding through a breathtaking landscape on horseback, camping under the stars and attending a golden eagle festival.

Megan notices that people often come back from such expeditions with a clearer idea of who they are and what they want from life.

'Often there's a reason why people sign up for a trip like that,' she says. *'They might have gone through something traumatic like a breakup or they may be trying to find the next step in their career. While out in nature and pushing themselves, they also get a chance to hang out with other people and be a part of something very special. Such trips and forays into the wilds can be life changing.'*

» Nature therapy

Although Megan thinks she was born with an "adventure gene", she doesn't believe you have to be an explorer or a survival expert to enjoy the power of nature.

'You certainly don't have to go running miles across mountains to enjoy the therapeutic effects that come from being outdoors. You get fantastic benefits from just taking the dog for a walk or being with friends in the park.'

RIDING HIGHS

Honorary Colonel of Derbyshire ACF Leigh Timmis reveals how he became a record-breaking round-the-world cyclist and adventurer.

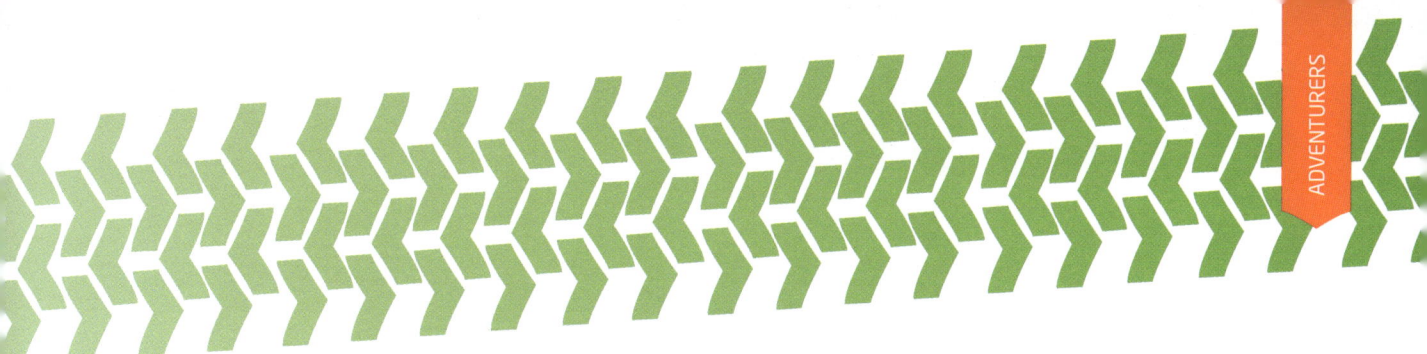

At 25 years old, Leigh Timmis had done everything he could to fit in with society's expectations of what it means to be successful.

'When I went to university I really focused on success; I was studying filmmaking and thought it was really important to get a first-class degree. With that, I might expect to come out of uni and get a great job and receive respect, rewards and good pay. So, while studying, I gave up the things I really loved in life, including cycling, to concentrate on doing well academically.'

Leigh subsequently graduated and landed a great job, but didn't find the expected sense of satisfaction in his success.

'My friends had moved away after university and I lived in a house with people I didn't really know. I then took on more and more work, which led to feeling stressed and overwhelmed.'

Overworked, lonely and sabotaging his own life, he was diagnosed with depression and sought help from a counsellor.

» Taste of adventure

That summer, along with two friends, Leigh acted on a whim and embarked on a month-long motorbike adventure across Iceland. The experience opened him up to a whole new world of possibilities.

'We motorcycled across these volcanic deserts, wild camped under the midnight sun, swam in volcanic waters and walked across glaciers. I felt so alive! Why would I want to go back to a life that was so unfulfilling when there was so much opportunity in the world?'

While Leigh's previous way of life had been governed by routine, this taste of adventure made him hungry for new experiences. Rediscovering his childhood passion for cycling, he set about his next big challenge.

» Journey of self-discovery

In 2010, Leigh cycled 44,000 miles across 51 countries on an epic solo expedition. It took him seven years and he gave himself a budget of £5 per day.

Pushing the limits of cycling and human endurance, he rode his bicycle in some of the most inhospitable places on Earth, but also across some of the most magnificent. The life-changing experiences he had along the way fostered a life-affirming belief that his fellow human beings were intrinsically friendly and kind.

'There were challenges, but I had to be brave and flexible enough to overcome them. I got very good at meeting new people and was often supported by the kindness of strangers I met along the road.'

'Having a challenge gave me a sense of direction, purpose and fulfilment. Every day I would wake up knowing I needed to find shelter and water but, after that, I could just see how things unfolded.'

'Imagine a life that had previously been so dark and unfulfilling, now being filled with that kind of excitement, spontaneity and adventure?'

» World-record attempt

On his return home, Leigh set himself another massive challenge. In 2018 he pedalled into the record books by becoming the fastest person to cycle across Europe, in a time of 16 days, 10 hours and 45 minutes. Cycling from the west coast of Portugal to the edge of Siberia – for 14 hours each day – he broke the previous world record by an astonishing eight days and seven hours.

'Before I set off I had to know what challenges lay ahead, how I was likely to react to them and what steps could be put in place to make sure they didn't prevent me from reaching my goal.'

'We wild camped under the midnight sun, swam in volcanic waters and walked across glaciers'

Leigh in training, on his cycling adventures, camping in the wilds and in uniform as Honorary Colonel of Derbyshire ACF

To this end, Leigh put together a team which included a fitness coach for a strong body, a nutritionist to help fuel his body for the challenges to come, and a physiotherapist to help him manage the physical demands of the feat. However, a physiologist from the sports science team at the University of Derby also advised him to take on the services of a psychologist.

'My response was: "This is all about legs and limbs. I'm not going to be falling in love out there". However, the physiologist said something to me that I now believe is the crux of any challenge, whether that is something you take on as a musician, dancer, parent, adventurer, sportsperson or artist. He said: "You can be the fastest cyclist in the world on the start line but it means nothing unless you have a mind that's strong enough to get you to the finish line".

'Out on the road, I quickly realised it was all about mental resilience. The body is able to keep going; it's the mind that wants to give up. When it's cold, wet and raining and you've been riding a bike for 14 hours a day for over two weeks, you start to wonder what it's all about. That's when you need mental strength.'

'Out on the road, I quickly realised it was all about mental resilience'

» Giving back

In November 2022, Leigh smashed the world record for the greatest distance cycled in seven days. The previous record was set in 1939 by long-distance cyclist Tommy Godwin and stood at 2179.66 miles. Leigh broke the record in the early hours of 13 November with a distance of 2230 miles. What made it so remarkable was that, for three days of this cycling challenge in Florida, conditions were affected by Hurricane Nicole.

As an ambassador for MQ (a leading UK mental health research charity), Leigh used the challenge to raise funds for mental health research. Knowing how much cycling, goal setting and adventure have positively impacted his own mental health for the better, his world record attempt was the perfect way to give back.

Leigh's motivation tips for any challenge

» Choose something based around an activity you love. However, if you don't know what to do, just take a step forward and choose something. You can always take further steps left or right later if it's not quite right.

» Be prepared to go out of your comfort zone, even if it feels difficult.

» Set yourself a target.

» Be your own project manager: set a timetable, plan what you will need and make lists. Get organised, create a schedule and learn time management skills.

» Try and predict what challenges lie ahead, how you are likely to react to them and what steps could be put in place to make sure they don't prevent you from reaching your goal.

» If you set yourself a physical challenge, remember to factor in recovery time. Create a lifestyle that will nourish the kind of growth you need to be able to meet the challenge.

» Imagine yourself at the finish line. When you feel like giving up or easing off, ask your future self at the finish line for advice. What would your future self tell you to do right now?

» In difficult moments, ask yourself what sort of person you want to be: one who gives up or one who gives it everything?

» Good sleep is the best tool you have for maximum performance.

» Bear in mind that behind any so-called "instant success" usually lie decades of hard work and failures.

» Don't just focus on the end achievement; enjoy the journey of getting there.

» During your challenge, focus on gratitude: get up in the morning and find three new things to be grateful for.

Go further

Scan the QR code to hear Leigh tell his story.

Leigh's story

INTREPID EXPLORER

Adventurer **Laura Bingham** reveals how the Army Cadets prepared her for a lifetime of adventuring in the furthest corners of the globe.

Asunción, Paraguay

Laura paddling in tough water in Essequibo

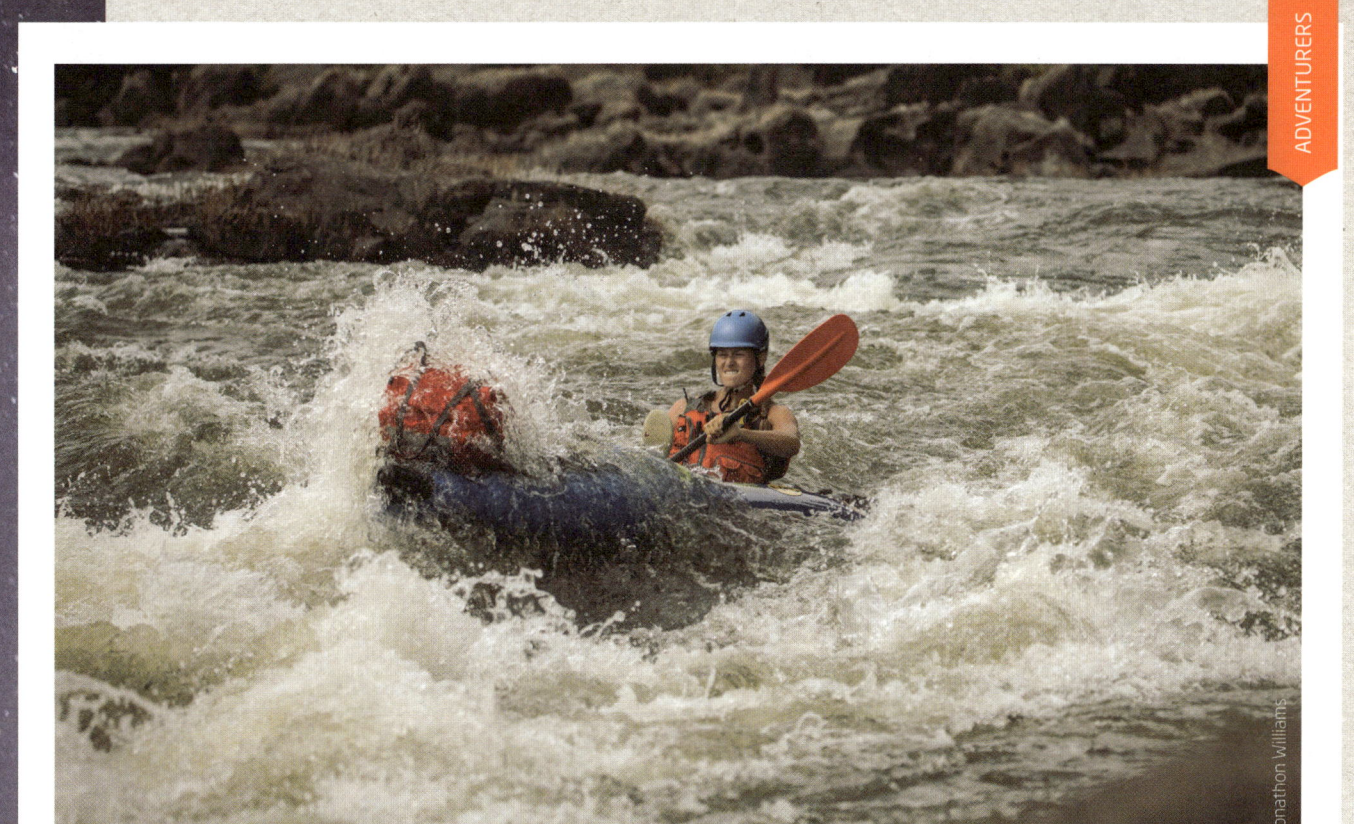

> 'Army Cadets builds resilience ... that's why I'm so comfortable with being uncomfortable'

She has sailed across the Atlantic, crossed South America penniless using only pedal power, and followed Guyana's longest river from source to sea by kayak. All this, and Laura Bingham is barely 30.

As if that were not enough, she has managed to combine her adventures with a growing family. She and husband Ed Stafford (himself a famous explorer and survivalist) have a six-year-old son Ran (named after polar explorer Sir Ranulph Fiennes) and twin three-year-old daughters Molly and Millie.

It makes for a charmingly chaotic interview, with the kids appearing regularly on screen to say hi. Laura spins the camera round to reveal a stunning natural vista, pointing out the ocean and mountains in the distance – they all decamped to Costa Rica in 2023, with the aim of building an exciting new life while the kids are still young.

» Cadet camaraderie

Cadets played a major part in Laura's early life. At the age of 15, she joined Z Company (once part of Hampshire and Isle of Wight ACF) in her hometown of Winchester. 'We met every Wednesday and we had amazing fun,' she recalls.

'I loved the camps, first aid, tuck shop, drill and shooting. These were things I was good at, and in a place where everyone was friends – unlike school, where I found the popularity dynamics hard to navigate. At Cadets, we all had a common aim and focus, and there was a real camaraderie in that.

'It also made us take responsibility for ourselves. We took huge pride in our uniform and, if anyone found out someone's mum had ironed it for them, we'd tease them.'

In 2009, at a national training camp in Norfolk, Laura joined 600 cadets and 200 adult instructors for a gruelling but thrilling week-long schedule of (deep breath) kayaking, climbing, mountain biking, go-karting, first aid, map reading, shooting, marching with heavy backpacks and overnight exercises.

Photo: Brandon Giesbrecht

Laura in the Essequibo

Photo: Jonathon Williams

'Cadets instilled an adventurous streak in me'

'Some parts weren't enjoyable at all,' she laughs, 'such as getting soaked on a recce mission in the middle of the night. But it felt good afterwards, because we'd all been through it together.

'It builds resilience, and that's why I'm so comfortable with being uncomfortable on expeditions now – I know I'll get through it quickly and it's something cool to talk about afterwards.'

» Adventures in South Africa

Laura grew up one of four siblings and, from the age of six, travelled to South Africa regularly to visit relatives. 'It instilled an adventurous streak in me,' she remembers. 'We went paragliding, white-water rafting and on safari. I even did a term of school out there.'

She admits, however, that in her early teens she became more indoorsy. 'I loved TV, and was especially into Hannah Montana!'

Laura as a cadet in 2009

Cadets got her out and about, but it was a difficult personal period in her late teens that pushed her towards extreme travel. *'It started out as self-punishment,'* she explains. *'The travels got bigger as my comfort zone expanded, until I found myself sailing across the Atlantic and leading the first guided expedition down the Essequibo River. And,'* she confesses, *'as the youngest of four, I loved the attention I received from carrying out these adventures.'*

» Bucket list

Aged 18, Laura wrote a bucket list of 83 things to cram into her lifetime. Some were standard: have an organised wardrobe, give blood. Others were decidedly more left field: meet monks, ride on the roof of a train in Ecuador (not advisable).

Several now have a big tick next to them. 'Learn a language' came into its own in Mexico, where Laura worked as an English teacher in 2014 while volunteering in jaguar conservation work for the government.

When it was time to go home, she realised she couldn't afford a plane ticket, so did her research and found a crew (two men and a cat called Cuba) who needed an extra pair of hands for the two-month sail back to Britain on a 38ft trimaran. *'My mum offered to pay for the flight, but I'd made up my mind,'* she laughs.

» Big bike ride

Next on the list came 'cycle across a continent'. Having learned Spanish, Laura plumped for South America. Her 7,000km, 164-day journey began in Manta on Ecuador's Pacific coast, passed through Peru, Bolivia and Paraguay, and culminated in the Argentine capital of Buenos Aires. It has since been immortalised in a series of books for young children, under the title of *One Girl and Her Bicycle*, written by Laura and illustrated by Laura Wall.

Even Sir Ranulph Fiennes described it as a *'risky undertaking'*, not least because she was travelling cash-free to raise awareness of extreme poverty. Inspired by the UK-based charity Operation South America, which provided homes and education for disadvantaged young women in Paraguay, she carried minimal equipment and relied upon what she could scavenge or trade, and on the kindness of strangers.

IIt was tough at times. *'I became a shell of a person until Paraguay. The other countries were less friendly and I felt like a burden to society, like I should crawl into a hole and disappear.'* I imagine that's how the homeless and people on benefits might feel.'

Despite the hardship, Laura learnt some important life lessons. *'I realised that what people need most, often more than money, is acknowledgement – to be seen.'*

Laura during the 630-mile expedition down Guyana's Essequibo River

'I'm not that good at anything, but I persevere'

Photo and inset: Pejman Zekavat

Laura, Ed Stafford and son Ran

Photo: Jon Williams

» Family life

In preparation for her Latin American quest, Laura contacted adventurer and survivalist Ed Stafford. She was considering making a documentary about her upcoming adventure and thought Ed would be able to give her advice about getting a production crew on board. Ed, a former Army captain, had starred in several TV documentaries and, like Laura, loved a challenge – he was the first person to walk the entire length of the River Amazon.

As they discussed Laura's plans for the epic bike ride, they realised they had a lot in common. They were engaged three months later and have been together for eight years. *'We are both whirlwinds. It's hard to find someone who understands why you'd want to do crazy things like leave everyone at home to paddle down a river for two and a half months.'*

❯❯ The Essequibo

Ran was eight months old when Laura got itchy feet. *'When you become a mother, your identity shifts and I didn't want to lose my former self; I had to do something that was true to me,'* she explains. Her own idea of crossing the Darién Gap, connecting Panama and Colombia, was rejected on the grounds that it was too dangerous due to flash flooding and guerilla warfare.

Ed had his own eye on the Essequibo, having explored parts of Guyana while filming his BBC series *Lost Land of the Jaguar*. He suggested it to Laura. *'When he told me I'd be one of the first people to go there, that was it – I was going,'* she says.

Her handpicked team of three included Ness Knight (Ran's godmother) and a comparatively new acquaintance, Pip Stewart. Together they found the river source by trekking through uncharted parts of the mountains and hacking their way through the jungle by hand – the first third of the Essequibo ticked 'find an untouched paradise' off her bucket list. At the end, where the river meets the Atlantic, they were paddling alongside gargantuan vessels in fearsome-looking waves.

They set a shining example to anyone, but especially young girls and women with dreams of adventure. *'The guy who met us off the plane wasn't expecting three girls,'* she laughs. *'But I choose my team on the basis that I would get along with them – you're pushed to your emotional limits on a trip like that.'*

❯❯ Make your own story

Laura's message to cadets, whatever their gender, is that they have the ability to make their own story. *'Even if you have no money or you're not from an amazing family, you can make your own connections,'* she says.

'You can always find reasons not to do things, but it's within your power to find solutions to the problems in front of you. Remember: excuses are what we tell ourselves to convince ourselves out of a dream.

'Don't be discouraged if you're not good at something. I'm not that good at anything, but I persevere. Just by doing that, you become the last person in the race when everyone else gives up – or your skills develop until you're the best.'

ADVENTURERS

'Excuses are what we tell ourselves to convince ourselves out of a dream'

Laura crossing a bridge over the Essequibo River in Guyana

ANNUAL CAMPS

2023 saw fantastic camps take place with all sorts of exciting activities for cadets to try. Here are some highlights – are you pictured?

» Colton Hills, The Royal School and The De Ferrers Academy CCF units at Nesscliffe

1

ANNUAL CAMPS

1. A cadet calm and ready to hit the field
2. Assessing the situation out in the field
3. A moment to chill and reflect
4. Receiving orders for what lies ahead in the field
5. A valuable moment of rest before the action continues

Photos: Kate Knight

89

» **Colton Hills, The Royal School and The De Ferrers Academy CCF units at Nesscliffe**

1

2

1. Surveying the scene
2. In the zone out in the field 3. Cadets and CFAVs looking out with intent as they await what comes next 4. In the zone and ready 5. CFAVs find time to reflect while out on exercise

Photos: Kate Knight

ANNUAL CAMPS

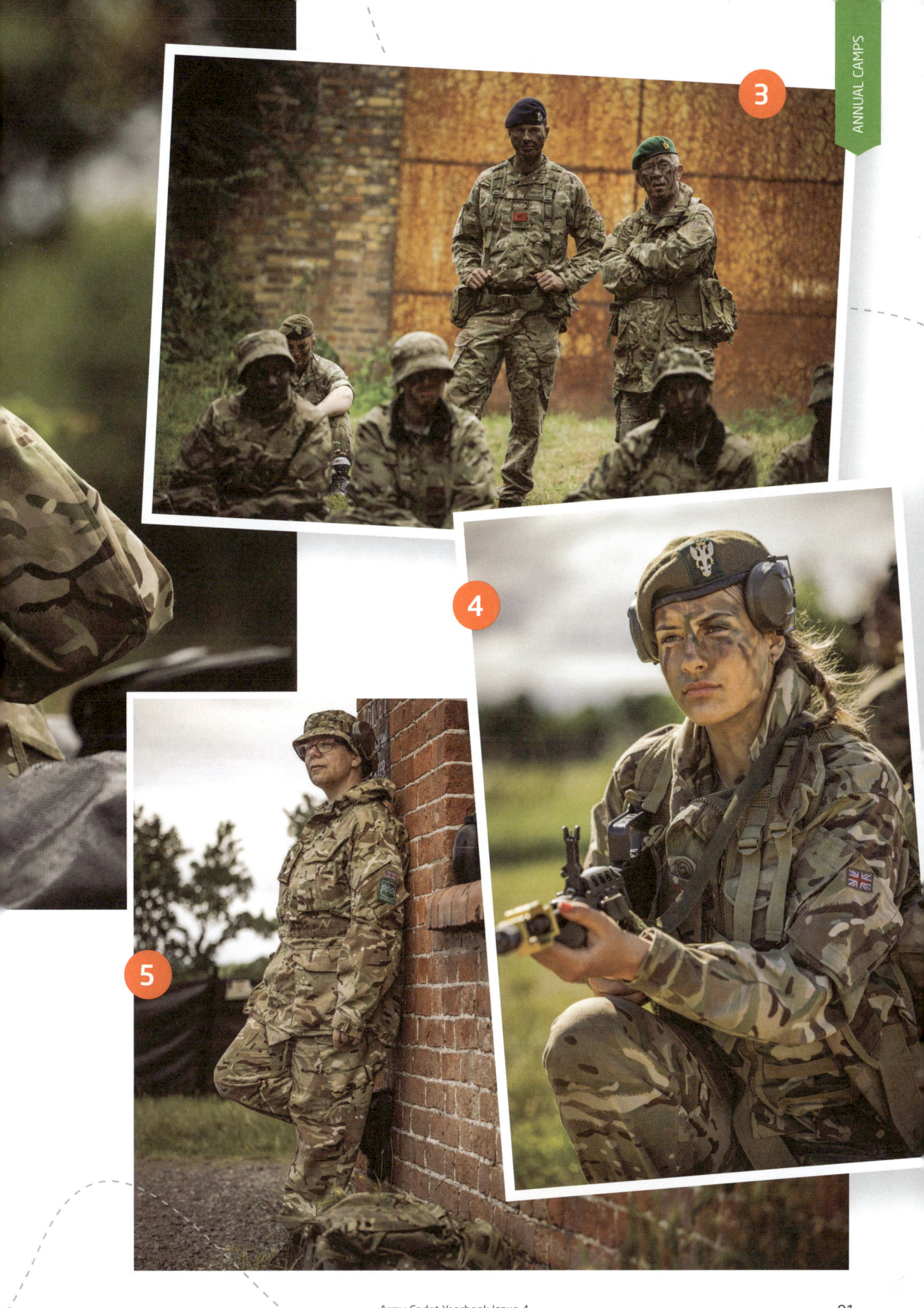

Army Cadet Yearbook Issue 4

Turn your passion into purpose at London's environmental college

We offer the perfect location for your studies with over 30 acres of gardens, a farm and over 200 acres of land spread across the capital. Boost your green skills and begin your career working outdoors.

Agriculture

Arboriculture and forestry

Wildlife and environmental conservation

Capel Manor College

Find out more about our full and part-time courses

capel.ac.uk

ANNUAL CAMPS

» Aldenham and Queens' CCF units at Crowborough, Sussex

1. Nothing beats paddle boarding in the sun! **2.** A different approach to fieldcraft, this time with paintball
3. Patrolling is always best in pairs

Photos: Priya Patel and Adam Simmonds

Army Cadet Yearbook Issue 4

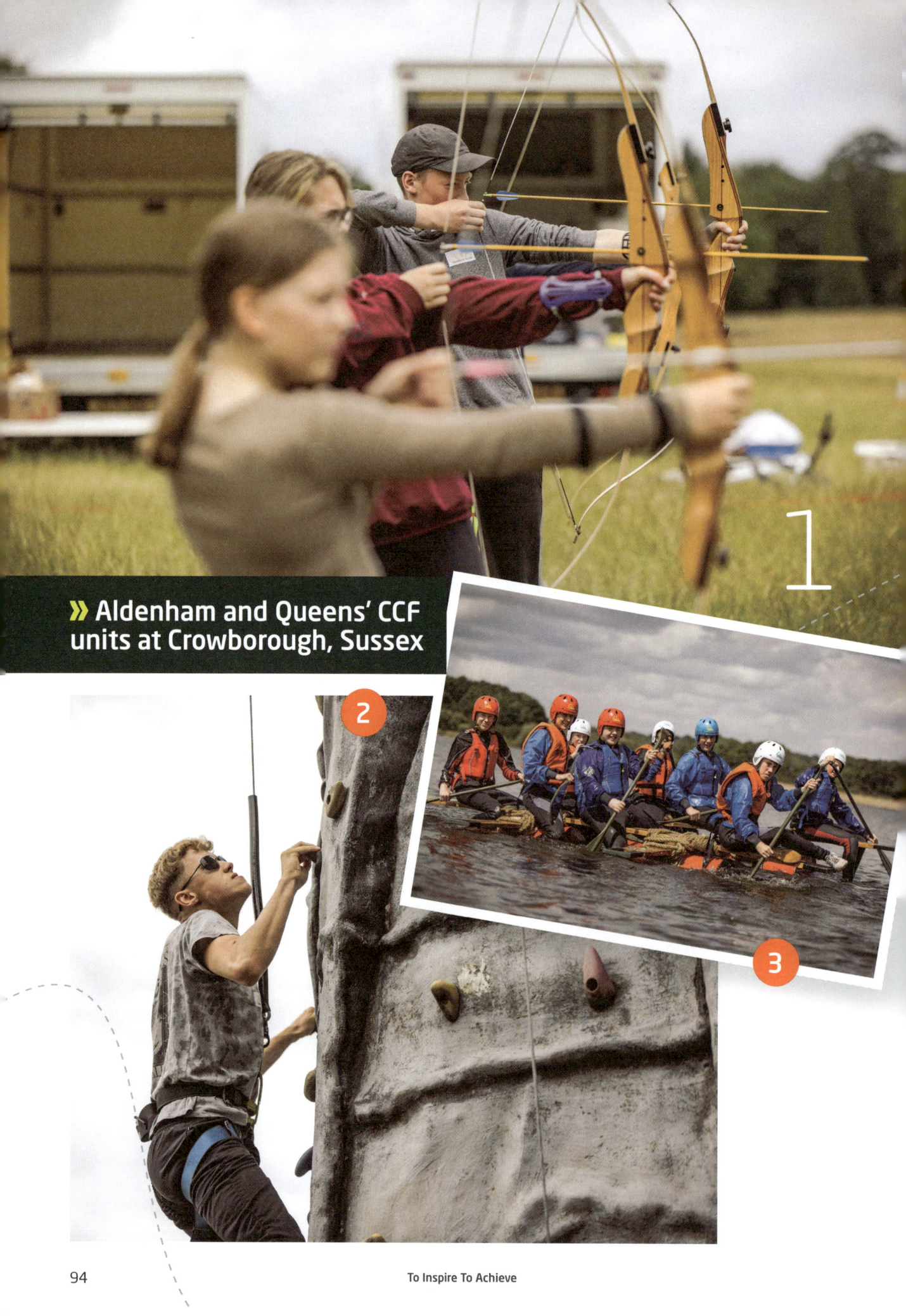

1

» Aldenham and Queens' CCF units at Crowborough, Sussex

2

3

94 To Inspire To Achieve

ANNUAL CAMPS

1. Marksmanship isn't always with a rifle – cadets aim with bows and arrows
2. Cadet tackling new heights
3. Cadets take a moment to pose while partaking in watersports
4. Instructor showing off their skills
5. Cadets take to their bikes to learn new skills on camp
6. One fieldcraft exercise received coverage from the National Media & Comms team

Photos: Priya Patel and Adam Simmonds

» City of London and North East Sector ACF at Castlemartin, Wales

1. Ready... Aim... Fire! Cadets get the opportunity to shoot clay pigeons **2.** Cadets climbing above their fears **3.** Nothing but smiles at annual camp **4. & 5.** Taking ICT to the next level with radios

Photos: Charley Doyle

ANNUAL CAMPS

3

4

5

97

1

2

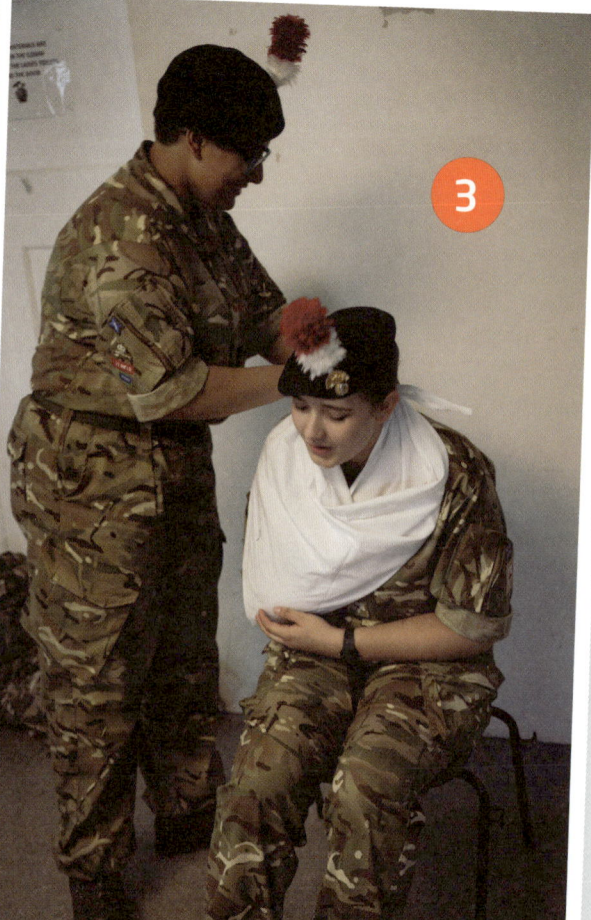

» City of London and North East Sector ACF at Castlemartin, Wales

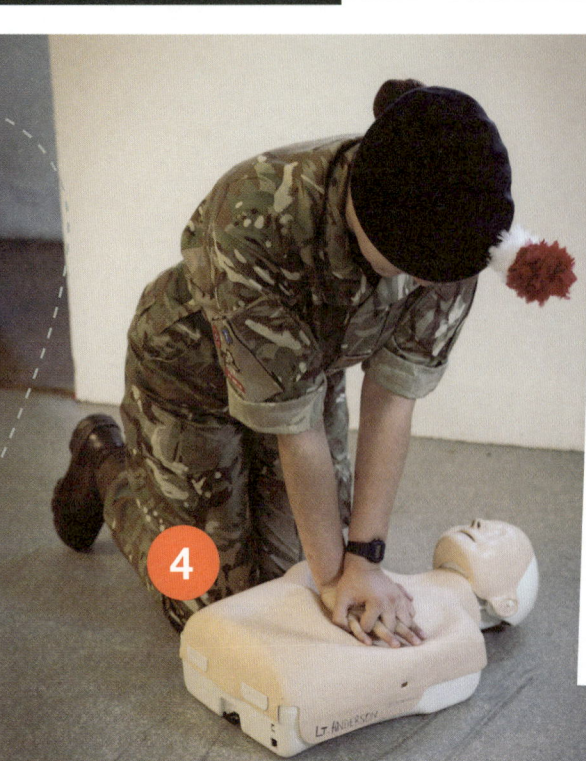

3

4

ANNUAL CAMPS

1. Cadet awarded 1-star pass badge **2.** A perfect aim **3. & 4.** Cadets learn valuable life skills including first aid **5.** Mountain biking taken to a whole new level **6.** Advancing to contact while out in the field **7.** Cadet mountain biking

Photos: Charley Doyle

Army Cadet Yearbook Issue 4

» **Greater London South East Sector ACF at Holcombe Moor, Manchester**

1

2

ANNUAL CAMPS

1. You meet all sorts of people – and animals – at camp! **2.** Cadets take their survival skills next-level by learning how to build field basha shelters **3.** Preparing to go out on exercise **4. & 5.** Cadets leave camp with various achievements and star passes

Army Cadet Yearbook Issue 4

>> **Greater London South West Sector ACF at Rollestone, Salisbury Plain**

1

ANNUAL CAMPS

1. Cdt LCpl Channing meeting Army Cadets National Ambassador Jordan Wylie MBE, post filming an exciting project
2. Camming up **3.** Non-stop smiling on exercise **4.** Patrolling to an ambush
5. Jordan inspects cadets

Photos: Charley Doyle

1

2

》 **Greater London South West Sector ACF at Rollestone, Salisbury Plain**

3

4

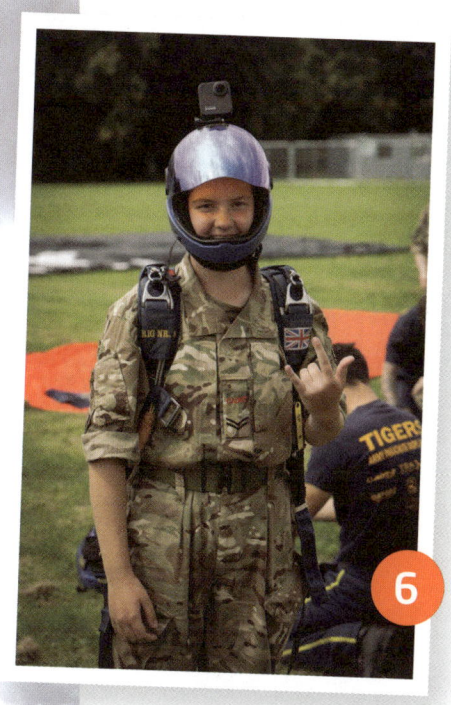

1. A cadet shows off their target after rounds of shooting **2.** Cadet lines up their target with the Cadet Small Bore Target Rifle **3.** Target sheets
4. CFAVs take a moment to pose for the camera
5. Cadets treated to a display of Army parachuting skills **6. & 7.** Some cadets faced their fears and went parachuting **8** The Tigers Parachute display team being presented to the Commandant

Photos: Charley Doyle

» **Middlesex and North West London ACF at Hankley Common and Aldershot**

1. A cadet in the field keeping their eye on the target **2.** Cadets in all-round defence **3.** Camming up **4.** Tactics in the field

Photos: Mitchell Allen

ANNUAL CAMPS

1

» **Middlesex and North West London ACF at Hankley Common and Aldershot**

2

3

108 To Inspire To Achieve

ANNUAL CAMPS

1. & 2. Cadets taking on the climbing wall as part of AT **3.** There's always time to capture the best moments at camp **4.** Cadets receiving a lesson **5.** Smiles after a day on the range **6** Annual camp is always a great opportunity to practise shooting skills

Photos: Mitchell Allen

109

CADETDIRECT
THE UK'S LEADING SUPPLIER OF CADET UNIFORMS & EQUIPMENT

Payments secured by **sage pay** | **VERIFIED by VISA** | **MasterCard SecureCode**
VISA Electron | VISA | MasterCard | Maestro

Kammo Tactical Cadet Assault Vest MTP KT001
£47.95

Delta Patrol Boot Full Leather
AB75 Brown
AB76 Black
FROM £39.95

Kammo Tactical Cadet Forces MTP Bergen, 70L
KT002
£52.95

ACF/CCF MTP Cadet Rank Slides
AA03RMC
£5.25

FREE
2024 CATALOGUE ORDER A COPY ONLINE

BULK DISCOUNTS – ORDER IN BULK FOR BIG SAVINGS

Army Cadet Basic Training Handbook - ACS
MB21CP
£9.99

Cadet Pocket Book (ACS Syllabus)
MB1
£11.95

ACF Adult CFAV flash
CFAV/ACF
£1.49

Proficiency Badges
FROM £0.89

VISIT **WWW.CADETDIRECT.COM**
TO SEE OUR FULL RANGE
Unit 4, Sybron Way, Crowborough, East Sussex TN6 3DZ
E-mail: orders@cadetdirect.com • Telephone: 01892 662 230
Contains images licensed under the Open Government Licence v3.0

ANNUAL CAMPS

1

>> **Leicestershire, Northamptonshire and Rutland ACF at Senta, Wales**

1. Cadets patrolling in the field
2. Cadets finding time to debrief each other **3.** Nothing but focus

Photos: Kate Knight

>> **Leicestershire, Northamptonshire and Rutland ACF at Senta, Wales**

1

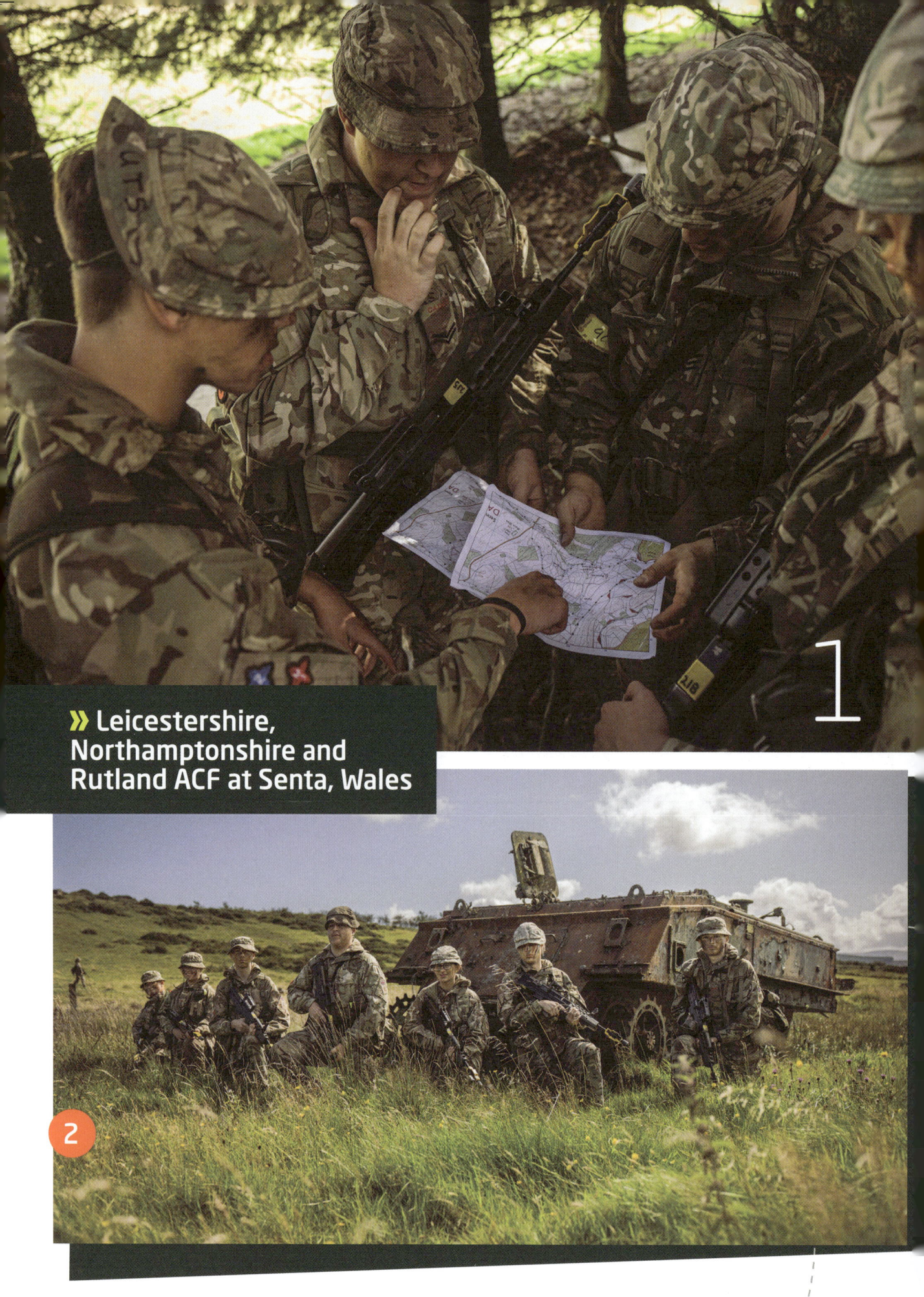

2

112   To Inspire To Achieve

1. Fieldcraft is a chance to practise navigation skills **2.** Cadets pose by a decommissioned armoured vehicle **3.** Cadets cross all sorts of obstacles out in the field **4.** Cadets building shelters while on exercise **5.** CFAVs planning what comes next

Photos: Kate Knight

ANNUAL CAMPS

❯❯ Wiltshire ACF at Crowborough, Sussex

1. Cadets take position for section attacks **2.** Smiles and friendship at camp **3.** Sunshine at camp boosts morale

ANNUAL CAMPS

1

» Argyll and Sutherland ACF at Chickerell, Dorset

2

3

1. Cadets take a moment to pose while completing their DofE Awards 2. Cadet beaming while doing AT 3. Cadet in the kneeling position while firing blank rounds on exercise

Army Cadet Yearbook Issue 4

Clywd & Gwynedd ACF at Swynnerton, Staffordshire

1. CFAV coaching a cadet after their rounds of live firing **2.** Cadet receiving recognition on camp **3.** Working together during a command task

» Cambridgeshire ACF at Beckingham, Nottinghamshire

1. Sliding into every adventure on camp **2.** Game face activated! **3.** Cadet showcases their musical talent **4.** Cadets patrol through long grass on exercise

Photos: SI Doug Stuart

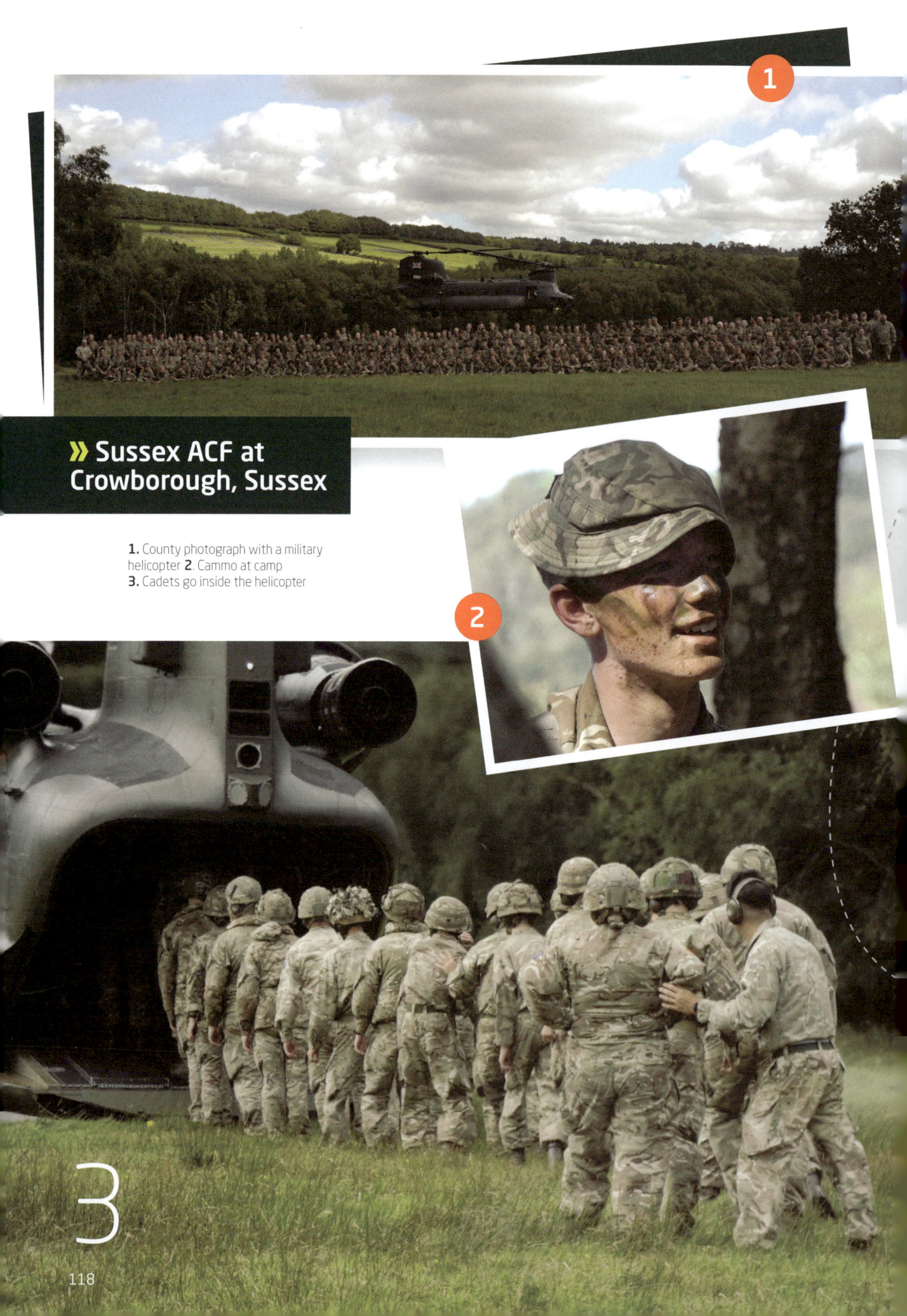

» Sussex ACF at Crowborough, Sussex

1. County photograph with a military helicopter **2.** Cammo at camp
3. Cadets go inside the helicopter

ANNUAL CAMPS

1

>> **Humberside & South Yorkshire ACF at Barry Buddon, Scotland**

2

3

1. & 2. Coasteering in Scottish waters **3.** Cadets white-water rafting

INSPIRATION

Meet inspirational cadets, former cadets, CFAVs and famous figures such as Dr Ranj Singh, who is advocating for a more inclusive style of masculinity.

The secretive world of the cyber-threat hunter

We sneak a peek into the secretive world of cyber security with **Lieutenant Olle Hawes, County Communications and Information Systems Officer**, E (HQ) Company, Sussex ACF, and head of cyber-threat hunting for Computacenter.

With the vast majority of business now taking place on smartphones, laptops, tablets and desktop computers, it has become more important than ever to take steps to prevent cyber criminals getting hold of accounts and data, and control of devices.

In his day job, 26-year-old Lieutenant Olle Hawes of E (HQ) Company, Sussex ACF is tasked with keeping businesses and organisations safe from the threat of cyber attacks and preventing unauthorised access to information stored online.

Olle and his team at Computacenter are on a daily mission to outwit cyber criminals and protect companies' devices and the services they access on them. We quizzed him to find out what qualities and skills are required to secure networks from intruders and combat malicious attacks on confidential and sensitive data.

» What does it take to succeed in cyber security?

All sorts of people enjoy careers in cyber security. It's helpful if you can focus and think clearly as you'll need to make sense of loads of complicated data, often under pressure. Sometimes the data can be intentionally flawed to distract from the real aim of the threat, so you need to think outside the box to identify the ultimate target and motive.

What is cyber security?

Any digital data – from a simple email between friends to a complex military defence system – needs to be protected from cyber criminals.

Cyber security ensures three things in relation to this data: the information is confidential and only accessible to authorised people; the information is uncompromised and in its original form; the people authorised to access it can do so without obstruction, interference or delay.

> 'Sometimes the data can be intentionally flawed to distract from the real aim of the threat'

Being good at cyber security takes teamwork – within an organisation and globally – so different skills and personality traits are all welcome, along with plenty of team spirit.

» How did you get involved in cyber security?

I first realised I enjoyed IT when I was a cadet with Signals Platoon. I'd intended to join the Army but an injury prevented me following that career path, so I opted for a degree in forensic computing and cyber security. While studying, I did a placement at Computacenter and returned to the company after graduation – I'm still here today! University is just one route into cyber security but there are many others, including lots of excellent apprenticeships.

» What does your role as head of cyber-threat hunting involve?

My team carries out various tasks. We look for signs that an organisation has been compromised in the past. Quite often, an organisation doesn't even realise it has been attacked and that information has been stolen, or that a threat is lying dormant in its systems.

We also run simulations to test security systems and carry out malware analysis, which involves running malware in a segregated environment to analyse it, reverse engineer it, potentially trace its source and prevent further threats.

My team also includes hunters who actively look for fresh threats in response to intelligence.

» Is cyber security a rewarding career?

It's a global issue and is always evolving because of geopolitical factors and the fact that cyber criminals are striving to stay one step ahead of us.

The motivations and attack methods vary so preventing and countering those attacks is interesting and rewarding, and likely to be in demand for a long time.

Sophos, a cyber-security software and service provider, recently reported 650,000 malware binaries (malicious software) a day – that's just one provider, so the challenge is huge.

» How can cadets get into cyber security?

Army Cadets offers lots of opportunities for cadets to learn about cyber security and there are dedicated initiatives to encourage more girls into cyber security careers.

The CyberFirst programme is a free nationwide scheme set up by the National Cyber Security Centre, part of Joint Communications HQ. If you are interested in CyberFirst courses, contact your county CIS officer or your detachment commander. The programme is a great introduction to cyber security and, if you want to progress further, there are bursary schemes and financial support available to support your studies.

» What role has Army Cadets played in your career?

My relationship with Army Cadets has continued throughout my career. While at university, I joined the University Officers' Training Corps and later became a CFAV before eventually becoming Communications and Information Systems Officer (CISO) for Sussex ACF.

Without Army Cadets, I wouldn't be where I am today. It gave me skills and confidence and my experience in Signals Platoon became the first step in my career. That's why I'm so passionate about introducing other cadets to IT and helping them engage with CIS programmes such as CyberFirst.

Olle (centre bottom row) and members of Sussex ACF Signals Platoon on annual camp in 2022

Photo: SIC Warren, Sussex ACF

Olle's top tips for staying safe in cyberspace

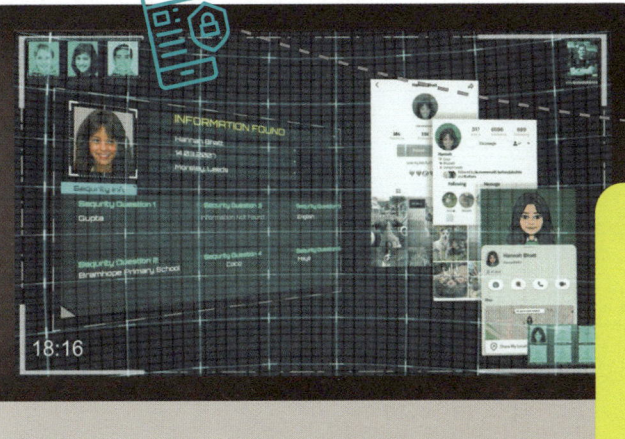

1. Use a password management programme instead of relying on the same passwords.

2. Always use multi-factor authentication – it's a free extra barrier to a security threat.

3. Never click links in unexpected texts or emails. Always go to the trusted website URL.

4. If you spot a possible online threat or scam, via text message, email or social media post, warn your friends and relatives and you could also make the police aware by calling 101.

5. Be aware that online personas may not be genuine and could hide a harmful agenda.

Go further

Scan the QR code to watch a Cyber Security Awareness video. Join National Ambassador Jordan Wylie and Brigadier Neville Holmes MBE, along with three cadets in the role of chasers, as they test the online security of some of our cadets.

Cyber security

FROM ARMY CADET TO ENTREPRENEUR

Youth politician, activist, author, entrepreneur and former cadet **Jeremiah Emmanuel BEM** shares his inspiring story.

Speaking at the Virgin Strive Challenge to raise money for Big Change

Jeremiah with entrepreneur Richard Branson

Former cadet Jeremiah Emmanuel has achieved more in his 24 years than some politicians accomplish in their lifetime. From overseeing a £25,000 budget as the Deputy Youth Mayor of Lambeth (age 13) to working alongside Bill and Melinda Gates (age 18), and to writing a book under Stormzy's publishing label (age 19), his philanthropic and entrepreneurial work has taken him around the world. He's even received a British Empire Medal in the honours list, which was presented by Lord-Lieutenant of Greater London Ken Olisa at the Tower of London.

Being involved in his local community has always been an intrinsic part of Jeremiah's life. He was just four years

'You might think something like drill has nothing to do with life in the outside world but it's fundamental to discipline'

old when he started campaigning in his south London community for a new school to be built in Brixton. As a young child he also got involved in educational campaigns, took an interest in politics and current affairs, and became an active member of his community.

When he was 12, Jeremiah joined the Army Cadets and scaled the ranks from cadet to cadet company sergeant major in his six years of service. He attributes many of the life skills that have aided his accomplishments to his Army Cadets training and experiences.

'I loved every single minute of my time at Army Cadets – it made me who I am today,' he says.

'Every aspect had a transferable skill. For example, you might think something like drill has nothing to do with life in the outside world, but it's fundamental to discipline and can help with concentration at school, being more organised and becoming more efficient.'

Living in London, the chance to escape the city in order to go on Army Cadets camps and expeditions was also appealing. Map reading and navigation were among his favourite activities and Adventurous Training experiences opened his eyes to the positive benefits of a change in environment.

'A lot of the people in my company grew up in council blocks and rarely experienced anything other than an urban environment. Army Cadets gave them a chance to leave London and see areas of the country they'd never experienced – it really changed their perspectives,' he says.

'This has inspired much of my charity work. I try to highlight that experiences in different environments can change young people's lives for the better.'

So, how did Jeremiah achieve so much at such a young age? On the following pages he shares some advice for young people with big dreams and reveals why activism is more important than ever.

Jeremiah's extraordinary CV

» **2004** Started campaigning with his mum for a new secondary school in Brixton

» **2011** Elected into the UK Youth Parliament as a MYP

» **2012** Became Deputy Youth Mayor of Lambeth and oversaw a budget of £25,000 to be spent on local projects

» **2013** Founded the BBC Radio 1 and 1Xtra Youth Council, which aimed to increase engagement between the broadcaster and young people

» **2015** Started his first company, EMNL. The youth consultancy agency worked with brands such as Nando's, Nike and Facebook to increase engagement with Gen Z

» **2017** Worked alongside Holly and Sam Branson at The Big Change Charitable Trust, an educational charity that helps kids

» **2017** Awarded the British Empire Medal for services to young people and the community

» **2018** Invited to be a Goalkeepers ambassador for the Bill & Melinda Gates Foundation, which involved accelerating progress toward achieving sustainable development goals

» **2020** Shared his story so far in his first book, *Dreaming in a Nightmare*, published by Merky Books

» **2022** Launched tech start-up Raffl, a new augmented reality app which pairs creators and influencers with brands to create outdoor experiences

» Achieving your dreams

'I once told a careers adviser that I wanted to become an author and she told me not to be too ambitious. A lot of people feel they can't achieve what they aspire to due to their current circumstances, environment or even the people around them and that's just not true. Anyone can achieve anything they want to achieve.

'I almost always end my public talks with the words: "Change is a word but we need to make it an action". In order to achieve something, you need to start putting in the action. The first step is to visualise everything on paper to help you figure out how you're going to get there. Use a pen and paper – not your phone. Do some research on people who've achieved your dream and work out what you need to do to get there.'

» Overcoming the fear of public speaking

'There have been times when I've been nervous before taking to the stage, but my experiences of commanding a squad in Army Cadets gave me the confidence to just do it.

'It's easy to overthink something like public speaking, and taking the first step is often the most daunting part. My advice is to think of it like marching – don't think about the end goal, just put one foot in front of the other – and instinct will guide you.'

» Why you should care about politics

'It's really important for young people to understand the influence they can have. The buying power of Gen Z is huge – it will climb to 40 per cent of all buying power by the end of 2023.

'If young people don't engage in politics, the policies and laws that will benefit them won't be achieved. We need to hold the people who represent us to account. For example, if you're not happy about something within your community, it's important to speak up and ask questions.

'The final reason is: why not? It can seem a bit boring and like nothing changes, but if you get involved at least you know there's a better chance of making an impact. I don't see any negatives in young people wanting to get involved in politics and making a difference in their communities.'

Speaking at WE Day alongside activist Karl Lokko at Wembley Arena

'My experiences of commanding a squad in Army Cadets gave me confidence'

» Redefining activism

'The word activism is quite broad. I've been described as an activist for most of my life, but activism means different things to different people. Someone who's part of a group that blocks roads is an activist, but so is the person who writes a letter to their local MP.

'Creativity provides a platform for activism. It can take it to new places and break it into different contexts and conversations. No matter what I do, I will always try to figure out a way to connect back to the community and the world around me.'

» Seek inspiration

'Not worked out what your dream is yet? Find the people who inspire you.

'I've been hugely inspired by Stormzy. At several different points in his career he thought of giving back. He knew he had a platform, so he used it to do good.

'Another person that inspires me is Akua Agyemfra, who works with Stormzy. She's an unstoppable driving force who helps pull together amazing ideas. You soon realise great people always have a great team. She was behind some of the amazing things Stormzy has done, such as establishing Merky Books (an independent book publisher for under-represented voices) and the Stormzy Scholarship (which provides financial support to black students at the University of Cambridge).'

Go further

Jeremiah's book, *Dreaming in a Nightmare: Inequality and What We Can Do About It*, is published by Merky Books and available now. £9.99.

Jeremiah was invited to be a Goalkeepers ambassador for the Bill & Melinda Gates Foundation

FIND YOUR OWN AMA

TV's **Dr Ranj Singh** has written a book called *How To Be A Boy And Do It Your Own Way* and is on a mission to encourage young people to be true to themselves.

Dr Ranj Singh, best known as a celebrity contestant on *Strictly Come Dancing* and for dispensing health advice on *Morning Live* on BBC One, is on a mission to ensure every young person feels confident in their own skin. His new book *How To Be A Boy And Do It Your Own Way* reads like an owner's manual for boys and young men, equipping them with the tools to help them look after their mental health, enjoy a positive body image and navigate peer pressure and bullying. It also unpacks gender stereotypes, leadership, allyship and respect for women, and reflects on what it takes to be kind and responsible in today's world.

Dr Ranj is out to reassure readers that there isn't one way to be a boy; what's important is to be true to oneself and kind to others. In exploring this he uses insights from his role as an NHS paediatrician, as well as extracts from high-profile personalities, including Army Cadets National Ambassador Jordan Wylie.

» Why did you write the book?

Just like many parents, carers and teachers, I feel concerned about the kind of messages boys and young men get through the media, especially social media. They are being bombarded with messages and images of how they should be, yet nobody is guiding them to how they could be. I wanted to help them discover who they really are, celebrate how brilliant they are and be the best version of themselves, which doesn't necessarily reflect the kind of masculinity they might see online or on screen.

» What do you hope readers get from the book?

There are themes of being confident, kind, compassionate and emotionally intelligent. I hope readers (of any age or gender) can take on those messages and feel they can be all of these things.

I'd like them to celebrate themselves but also other people. There's a thread in the book about kindness and being a decent human being and about showing respect for others' individuality and diversity.

No matter who the reader is, their background, abilities, or where they're from, I hope they take away positive messages that don't always get aired. I'd like it to give them permission to be themselves – and to be brilliant!

» How did gender stereotypes affect you when you were growing up?

We talk a lot in the book about expectations. These might be expectations of boys based on their gender, culture and race. I come from quite a traditional Indian background and, like in many other cultures, boys are expected to behave in a certain way – to be the leaders, the macho ones, the ones in charge. If somebody had told me when I was younger that I could be whatever I wanted to be, without pressure to be a certain way, I think I would have been happier.

INSPIRATION

'You are brilliant just as you are so celebrate it and show everyone'

ZING!

I wish I'd had this book when I was young. Perhaps I would have had the confidence to say: 'Hold on a second, I don't feel like this. I feel different from my friends and other boys. I'm not into the same things.' Nobody was telling me that was okay.

I wish someone had tapped me on the shoulder and said: 'You're doing okay. You don't have to change for anyone. You don't have to be a particular way. You are brilliant just as you are so celebrate it and show everyone.'

I didn't learn that until I was in my thirties. The main thing I want to tell people is: find your own amazing!

›› How can cadets be allies to each other?

First and foremost, you need to educate yourself about different kinds of people. You can help others by listening, talking and learning. Let other people take the lead in the conversation and sit back and learn from them.

The best way to be an ally is to understand where other people are coming from. You might not realise it but you may be in a relatively privileged position compared to someone else. That's not inherently a bad thing but, to be a good ally, it's important to listen, try to understand, educate yourself and use whatever privilege you have to lift up others.

You can use whatever is in your toolbox to help you do that. That could be volunteering, standing up for somebody or just being there for another person. Fundamentally, it's about being a decent person. We call it allyship. When you are part of a team, an organisation or a collective of some kind the whole point is to support each other and help each other achieve more.

›› What makes a good leader?

There's no single way to be a good leader as different kinds of leadership work in different situations. If you are a leader, the first thing to realise is that you are part of a team and it is not all about you – it's about you and everyone around you, collectively. Good leaders don't just tell people what to do; they recognise the qualities and capabilities of those around them and know how to use those skills for the collective good.

Good leaders also know how to listen and are understanding, empathetic and flexible. They should be able to admit when they are wrong. As a leader, it's important to bear in mind that you are not perfect, that you have limits and might make mistakes.

'Good leaders don't just tell people what to do; they recognise the qualities and capabilities of the people around them'

How To Be A Boy And Do It Your Own Way, published by Wren & Rook, is out now.

Dr Ranj's advice on how to be a good ally

- Speak out when others make jokes about girls (sexism)
- Speak out when others make jokes about LGBTQ+ people (homophobia/biphobia/transphobia)
- Speak up when someone gets treated differently because of their skin colour (racism)
- Support someone when they are being bullied – let a teacher or other responsible adult know
- Don't tease girls about their bodies or things like periods
- Don't make fun of anyone who is into things that are different from what others consider the norm
- Check in with someone after they've had an upsetting experience and offer them help

» Why is Pride Month important and how can we ensure everyone feels welcome?

It's important that everyone learns about Pride. The great thing is that a lot of young people *do* know about it and are more open, understanding and savvy than some older members of society – so can lead by example.

Pride is important all year round but many celebrate it in June during the lead up to the Pride in London parade. If you are a member of the LGBTQ+ community, Pride Month is your time to show the world how brilliant you are; it's a time to celebrate yourself and shine. It's an opportunity to showcase the community and how wonderful it is.

As for allies, when you take part in Pride celebrations, remember you are there as guests. You have been let into the space and you should respect that and use your allyship to make things better.

Recognise that the LGBTQ+ community is at a disadvantage in so many ways. You may not have the same struggles as members of that community, but you can help by making the Cadets experience as welcoming and wonderful as possible.

» What's your advice for cadets struggling with low mood?

Any young person who doesn't feel their best needs to know it's normal to feel like that, and that they are not alone. When you're young you're still trying to work out who you are and where you fit in the world. In addition, there are lots of things going on in the brain and body that can compound those feelings.

It's important to remember that no one feels like that forever. If, however, you're unable to manage your feelings by yourself, reach out and talk to someone. You may not find that person straight away; it may take a couple of goes to find the right person but there will be somebody willing and able to support you.

» What are your top tips for building self-confidence?

When we're in a funk and not feeling our best we forget the great things about ourselves. We get preoccupied by a negative viewpoint and the negative voice in our head, and fixate on the things we don't like, forgetting the things we do like about ourselves.

Try to change your viewpoint. Ask yourself: *'What are the things I do love about myself? What are the things that have gone well for me?'*. Try to find the positive wherever you can.

If, however, you're really struggling and it's getting in the way of you enjoying life and doing the things you want to do, you do need to speak to someone and get some help.

Go further

Dr Ranj recommends learning about the LGBTQ+ community and speaking to LGBTQ+ people about their experiences.

As part of an ITV series, *A Letter To My 14-Year-Old Self*, celebrating the LGBTQ+ community, he reflects on his own journey of self-acceptance, plus his optimism about future generations. Scan the QR code to watch the video.

INSPIRATION

'It's fantastic to be asked to not only represent the Cadets but the Royal Family too'

Cdt RSM Hope Relph alongside High Sheriff Jennifer Duke and Lord-Lieutenant Mohammed Saddiq

HIGHEST HONOUR

Cdt RSM Hope Relph of Somerset ACF reveals what it's like to be a Lord-Lieutenant's Cadet.

A Lord-Lieutenant's Cadet is a representative of the cadet forces to the British Royal Family and acts as an aide to the Lord-Lieutenant of their county. To find out more about what the role entails we caught up with 17-year-old Cdt RSM Hope Relph from Taunton, who is a Lord-Lieutenant's Cadet in Somerset.

» Tell us about your Army Cadets career?

I joined when I was 12 years old. My dad was (and still is) a CFAV and my brother was a cadet and I wanted to get involved. I've now passed the whole syllabus. I've completed my Bronze and Silver DofE Awards and I'm currently doing my Gold. I've done adventurous training and fieldcraft training courses too.
When I turned 17 last year I became RSM, which means I'm in charge of the whole of the Somerset ACF, which is approximately 600 cadets. If there are any problems, I sort them out. I also go on visits to different camps. It's a really busy job and involves lots of planning, but I really enjoy it.

» How did you become a Lord-Lieutenant's Cadet?

Last September I was told I'd been put forward by my Company Commander for the position of Lord-Lieutenant's Cadet. It was a complete surprise. I was so honoured and it felt like all the hard work I'd put in over the years had paid off. It's such an amazing opportunity. I had to go to the Lord-Lieutenant's office for an introduction with the other nominated cadets, and we then had our investiture in October.

Above: Cdt RSM Hope Relph receiving the Best ACF Team Award on behalf of Somerset ACF at Cosford

» What are your main duties in the role?

I assist the Lord-Lieutenant of Somerset at civic and military occasions and represent the cadet forces to the British Royal Family. In Somerset we have five Lord-Lieutenant's Cadets in total, one from each cadet force.

One of my first events was Remembrance Day. I joined other local dignitaries like the mayor and the chief of police. More recently, I went to the British Empire Medal ceremony in Taunton.

Cdt RSM Hope Relph pictured in the city of Wells on official duties

'It's given me so many new skills and really built my confidence'

The Lord-Lieutenant's office usually emails me a few months in advance of an event and asks if I'd like to attend. I think I've been to every one they've invited me to, because I really want to make the most of the experience. I'm lucky that my dad is happy to drive me to most events, as I don't yet have my licence, and college allows me to leave classes early if there's somewhere I need to be.

» What do you enjoy about it?

The opportunities are amazing. It's fantastic to be asked to not only represent the Army Cadets but also the Royal Family. I meet so many people who are willing to give cadets opportunities and that's so important because we're a youth organisation. The experiences we are given we can take forward into our lives, no matter what we go on to do. On a personal level, it's given me so many new skills and really built my confidence. Before I joined the Army Cadets I was really shy and quiet. Now I have overwhelming confidence and feel like I can go on and achieve what I want to do.

» What's been your most memorable moment?

Meeting Queen Camilla at the opening of the Royal Osteoporosis Society's new offices in Bath. I was a bit nervous beforehand but at these events I always have adults from the Army Cadets with me who offer support and help me to prepare. The Queen was really lovely and we had a brief chat. She's the Colonel-in-Chief of The Rifles and in Somerset ACF we wear The Rifles cap badge, so it was a good conversation starter.

» What would you like to do as a future career?

I'm at college studying nursing and my plan is to get my degree and go on to become an Army Officer Nurse. What I've achieved as a cadet has definitely inspired my career and given me lots of different skills, including a qualification in First Aid at Work.

INSPIRATION

Cadet RSM Hope Relph with Lord-Lieutenant's Cadet FS Alex Day, RAFAC, and Lord-Lieutenant Mohammed Saddiq

» Would you recommend joining the Army Cadets?

I think everybody should be encouraged to do it. We learn so many things including first aid, fieldcraft, adventurous training, navigation, expeditions and loads of essential life skills.
I think it brings out the best in people. It's truly amazing how many young people are shy and have low self-esteem, but then they join the Army Cadets and we help build them up to be the person they want to be, and give them the opportunities to do what they want to do.

Cadet RSM Hope Relph recognised at the 2023 Pride of Somerset Youth Awards

CHAMPION CADET

Cdt RSM Josh Siggers reveals how he went from being a shy teenager to becoming Champion Cadet and a banner bearer at the coronation of King Charles III.

It has been quite a year for 18-year-old Cadet Regimental Sergeant Major (RSM) Josh Siggers from Kent. Having attained the Army Cadets' top rank, in April he beat tough competition to win the Claire Shore Trophy and take the Champion Cadet title at Cadet Training Centre (CTC) Frimley Park. Then in May, he was selected for the ultimate honour: to march carrying the Army Cadets banner during the coronation of King Charles III. He revealed what it was like and what's next for him.

To Inspire To Achieve

» How did your Army Cadets journey start?

I joined Ashford Tobruk Detachment, part of Kent ACF, in 2017 at the start of year eight. My elder brother was a cadet and loved it, so my parents were very supportive of me following him. At that point in my life, I was quite reserved and nervous and I definitely lacked discipline. For example, in my personal admin, I didn't take a lot of pride in what I did or what I looked like. I didn't carry myself with a sense of purpose, but that has all changed. The Army Cadets taught me to care about how I present myself, to set myself high standards and meet them – and expect the same of others.

» How did the Army Cadets equip you for life in general?

I think the Army Cadets is unique in that it offers you the opportunity to grow up and develop into a better person. It points you in the direction of being self-sufficient while also training you to work as part of a team. The skills I've learnt that translate into the real world are respect, discipline, the ability to follow instructions, and how to lead others and give orders. Above all, it's taught me to set an example.

> **'Army Cadets taught me to care about how I present myself, to set myself high standards and meet them'**

» You're a Regimental Sergeant Major (RSM). What does that mean?

It's the pinnacle of a cadet's career, a representation of what everyone should aspire to be. You need role models when you start out, and that's what an RSM is. The support I got from instructors and senior cadets on my own journey was so important. Being trusted by adults to lead other cadets has been a massive confidence boost to do better and be better, both for them and for myself.

Josh representing the Army Cadets as banner bearer at the coronation of King Charles III in London

Rehearsing alongside other banner bearers at CTC Frimley Park

What are your responsibilities as an RSM?

I spend weekends working with adult instructors, helping them take lessons and supervise. My experience as a cadet can be used to add a different perspective to situations other cadets might go through in the classroom or in the field. It's not to berate or shout, but to show cadets what's possible, how to do things correctly and be better. No cadet gets things right first time around and it helps to know we all start in the same place. Trying your hardest is always going to be the right answer.

What was the competition like to win Champion Cadet?

There were about 30 competitors, split equally between CCF and ACF, with every county sending at least one. We were tested on every aspect of our cadet knowledge – first aid, navigation, shooting, stalking – not all of which I'd done before, and in an environment I wasn't familiar with. Building camouflage onto my helmet, firing and manoeuvring – those were new to me. It was certainly challenging, although the basic skills I'd learnt previously in the Army Cadets helped.

How did you feel when you won?

The scoring system was kept secret, so it was impossible to tell how we were doing. It came as such a surprise when I won. It meant everything. The staff put so much faith in me: having seen my progress over the years, they thought I could do it. My County had never won before, so my win tells Kent cadets they are of a standard where they can go there and represent Kent at a national level – and win. I like to think I've given them the confidence that any of them can do exactly what I did, because my experience as a cadet began in the same place as theirs. You can start off undisciplined, scared even, and yet reach the heights of winning Champion Cadet. That's what means the most to me. It makes me proud.

As if it couldn't get any better, along came the coronation …

The week after winning, my OC got a call asking if they would like to send a representative to carry the standard at the coronation, and I was chosen because of my Champion Cadet status. I was stunned. My detachment was really excited and my mum cried – it made her realise how all the Army Cadet activities over the years were paying off. I don't think my dad believed it until he saw me on TV!

From the moment we got the call to when we started rehearsals, every day after school I polished my dress shoes and my Sam Browne belt, and put Brasso on my buckles and the lint roller on my peaked cap. I wanted to make sure I looked my best.

What was the build-up like?

I went to the CTC Frimley Park on the Tuesday for rehearsals – banner drill and marching in step. I then went to London where I took part in the overnight rehearsal until 4am alongside the members of all the armed forces. For the actual event, we marched from the banks of the Thames to the Foreign and Commonwealth Office, our hub for the day.

At Parliament Square we gave the Royal Salute as the King went past. He looked at us and smiled in acknowledgment, which was a proud moment. We had a break, then came back out for when the King departed and marched to Westminster Bridge. People were lined up, screaming and cheering. It felt really good.

What's next for you?

I'm doing A Levels in politics, chemistry and physics. My brother joined the forces, but that's not my path. I still want a job where I'm giving something back, so I'll be joining Kent Police. I want to focus on conflict resolution and developing my communication skills. In the Army Cadets good communication is definitely helpful, but you don't learn it directly – it comes from all the little experiences. These skills will be invaluable when I join up. Once I'm settled, I would like to come back to the Army Cadets as an adult instructor; I get a lot of pride and satisfaction in helping people.

> 'No cadet gets things right first time around and it helps to know we all start in the same sort of place'

INSPIRATION

Ranked among THE BEST

What does it take to be a cadet regimental sergeant major (RSM)? We chart the rise of two cadets who've reached the highest rank in Army Cadets.

» Ashanti Mai Holden, Cadet RSM of Yorkshire (North and West) ACF

Ashanti arrived in Yorkshire from the Philippines in 2016. Just six years later at the age of 18, she was appointed Cadet RSM of Yorkshire (North and West) ACF with responsibilities which included commanding up to 400 cadets in county parades. Ashanti attained the skills and qualifications needed for the role (something very few cadets achieve), despite having to face additional challenges.

'My brother joined Cadets before me and he loved it so much I decided to join too,' she says. 'I hadn't been in the UK long then, so there were lots of things I had to get used to: a new home, new school and new friends. Cadets provided a community and helped me find my place in a new country.

'I've absolutely loved the opportunities the Army Cadets has given me and I've made the most of every single one. I've loved raising money for charity, climbing mountains and even playing rugby – which is quite something for a four-foot-nine girl.'

Ashanti's Detachment Instructor, Lewis Wilde of Northallerton Detachment, said: *'It's been amazing watching Ashanti transform from a shy newcomer to the outstanding cadet she is now. She is respected by all who meet her and I'm immensely proud of her achievements. She brings sunshine and positivity to the detachment, as well as huge amounts of self-discipline and commitment to any task.'*

'I've absolutely loved the opportunities the Army Cadets has given me and made the most of every single one'

INSPIRATION

Ashanti Mai Holden, Cadet RSM of Yorkshire (North and West) ACF inspecting cadets

Photos: Richard Dougherty

Army Cadet Yearbook Issue 4

County Regimental Sergeant Major Instructor Austin Butler with his cadet counterpart Ashanti – both with pace sticks that only a very few are qualified to hold

'Cadets provided a community and helped me find my place in a new country'

» The route to cadet RSM

To be eligible for the role of Cadet Regimental Sergeant Major (RSM), cadets must first complete the Master Cadet Course. The course is open to 4-star cadets over the age of 16, with a minimum rank of sergeant, who have completed fieldcraft as a progressive subject and qualified on the Senior Cadet Instructors' Cadre (SCIC).

To be eligible for the Master Cadet Course, cadets should also have passed a weapon handling test on the L98A2 Cadet GP Rifle and, among several additional recommendations, are expected to have a good understanding of section battle drills and be fit enough to complete the physical elements of the course.

On completion of the Master Cadet Course, cadets can be considered for appointment as a cadet RSM, at the discretion of the ACF County Commandant. Only one company sergeant major (CSM) in a county will be selected to be its cadet RSM. They are the most senior cadets in the ACF and often take on ceremonial duties in the local area.

Reflecting on Ashanti's success, Commandant Fred Owen is in no doubt about the excellent example she has become and the inspiration she offers fellow cadets.

'Ashanti demonstrates what young people can achieve. She has risen to the very highest pinnacle for a cadet. Since joining, she has embraced every opportunity given to her. As well as mastering the English language, she has become a fantastic ambassador for mental health by supporting her fellow cadets throughout the pandemic. I'm delighted she has succeeded in achieving the rank of Regimental Sergeant Major.'

County Regimental Sergeant Major Instructor, Warrant Officer Class 1 Austin Butler, is also impressed with Ashanti's progression within Army Cadets.

'Ashanti commands the respect of all the cadets and shows the qualities needed to be a remarkable regimental cadet sergeant major. She has a positive outlook in everything she takes on and inspires her fellow cadets to be the very best they can be.'

Ashanti hopes to join the Royal Corps of Signals when she finishes her education, and will no doubt excel in a career in the British Army.

» Erin Donovan, Cadet RSM of Merseyside ACF

Erin joined Merseyside ACF in 2018 and, over the years, has embraced the full Army Cadets experience. From daunting early adventures such as first trips away from home, to fine-tuning her training on the Master Cadet Course, Erin has taken the positives from every occasion.

'I found Cadets engaging right from when I was attending camps as a junior cadet, so the years have flown past,' she reflects. 'It was a huge milestone when I reached the stage of being able to advance beyond 4-star and attend the Master Cadet Course at Frimley Park.

> **'As cadet RSM you need to hold yourself to the highest standards'**

'The course was one of my most enjoyable Cadets experiences – I was fully immersed in the battle picture of every section attack. It was a great chance to put my knowledge into practice, supported by the CFAVs and regular soldiers who helped us appreciate the importance of leadership and teamwork – even when we were tired and fed up.'

The honour of being selected for the role of cadet RSM brings with it a responsibility to uphold and reflect the core values of Army Cadets, something Erin recognised and took pride in.

'I was promoted on my annual camp, so was able to make the most of the position immediately by getting involved with training and making sure the cadets had the best experience possible. Since then, I've also visited units around my County, which provided amazing experiences and insights into best practice which I've been able to take back to my own unit.

'As cadet RSM, you need to hold yourself to the highest standards in order to set an example for other cadets to follow, and to demonstrate your own integrity and belief in the core values of the Army Cadets. I've developed as a cadet by constantly reflecting on my actions and decisions, and by being open to new approaches. I try to support others to do the same.'

At the time of the interview, Erin was approaching the end of her time in the Army Cadets but was looking forward to transferring her skills and qualities to a career in medicine.

'The medical profession shares many values with the Army Cadets: those of compassion, inclusiveness, integrity and respect. I've developed all those in Cadets – along with skills in leadership, confidence-building, time management and teamwork – and I'm looking forward to applying them to my future career.'

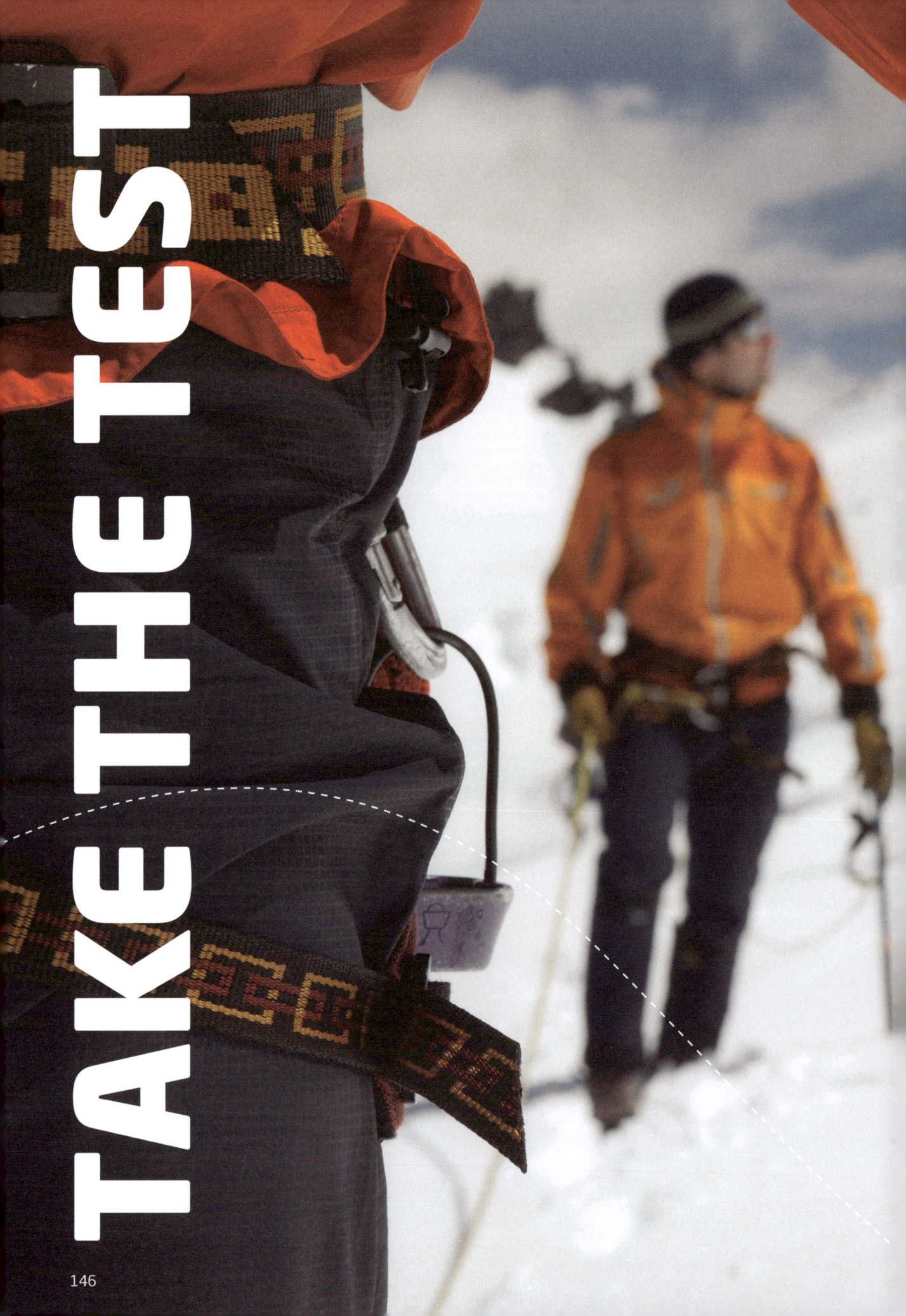

TAKE THE TEST

How much do you know about military fitness, annual camps, navigation and administering first aid in freezing conditions? Time to find out ....

TAKE THE TEST
MILITARY FITNESS

Military fitness expert **Leo Walker** of Who Dares Gyms puts your workout knowledge to the test.

CEO and founder of Who Dares Gyms Leo Walker trains people in military-style workouts at his gym on Bournemouth Beach, which he co-runs with Jason Fox (star of Channel 4's *Who Dares Wins*) and Tom Beaver.

Drawing on his background as a former Royal Marines Commando Training Instructor and Special Forces Instructor, Leo helps people of all ages and walks of life to experience military-style workouts.

In a career spanning 20 years in the armed forces, Leo has had to be fit in order to carry out missions in all kinds of outdoor environments – from mountains and deserts to jungles and the Arctic. The workouts he creates focus on functional fitness rather than conventional gym-based exercise.

'Functional fitness is a life skill,' he explains. 'It's about your body being at the absolute maximum peak of

TAKE THE TEST

Jason Fox, star of Channel 4's Who Dares Wins

'If military personnel aren't at peak fitness it can be catastrophic'

functioning. If military personnel aren't at peak fitness it can be catastrophic and compromise the mission.'

Being at peak functional fitness means having enough strength, mobility and power to deal with any situation that might arise.

'We've got weights, bars, dumbbells and cardio machines at our beach gym, but we also focus on climbing over wooden walls, pushing tyres and crawling under cargo nets,' says Leo.

'Functional fitness is all about preparing yourself physically and mentally so you can perform effectively and with confidence in any surrounding and situation (including emergencies). You won't achieve that simply by doing a generic weight session at the gym.'

Leo also runs Op Commando weekends, which are open to those who want to join the forces as well as curious civilians keen to find out more about what military training really entails.

'All kinds of people attend those weekends because they get to experience what real-life physical training is like for members of the armed forces. Some participants are cadets or those intending to join the military, but we also get people who have been prohibited from signing up because of their age or medical conditions.'

Leo and the Who Dares Gyms team have chosen ACCT UK as a key charity partner.

'We wanted to support the Army Cadets because it teaches young people to have confidence and show respect for others. That's something being in the Marines taught me: show respect to people because everyone has something to contribute.'

TEST

1 Which fluid is best for hydration?

A. Fruit juice.

B. Sports drink.

C. Water.

2 What's a good schedule for an average person who wants to take up running?

A. Two to three runs a week at a distance of three to five kilometres.

B. Run every day for as long a distance as you can manage.

C. Run once a week for 10km.

3 In a military-style workout, which exercises build strength?

A. Core and flexibility exercises like yoga and Pilates.

B. Progressive body-weight exercises.

C. Cardio activities such as running.

4 How do you make a training programme progressive?

A. Follow a balanced workout plan that steadily increases in intensity, integrated with plenty of rest, recovery and mobility.

B. Take advantage of advanced workouts which promise to push you to your max from the get go.

C. Allow the body to acclimatise and adapt in the first few months of the training programme by sticking to familiar exercises performed at the same intensity.

5 To achieve a strong core, which areas of the body should you train?

A. Glutes and lower back.

B. Abdominal muscles, shoulders and glutes.

C. Abdominal muscles and lower back.

See opposite for Leo's answers »

Southampton FC training with Who Dares Gyms

TAKE THE TEST

'Functional fitness is about preparing yourself physically and mentally'

ANSWERS

1. C The best way to achieve pure hydration of the body is by drinking water. As long as you're consuming sufficient amounts of vitamins and minerals throughout the day (through a balanced diet) you shouldn't need to consume any other forms of liquid, such as sports drinks, to stay hydrated.

2. A Knowing how far and how often to run is a difficult question to answer, as it's dependent on your fitness background and goals. A general rule is to stick to two or three runs a week, at a distance of three to five kilometres. If you look to progress beyond that, ensure you raise your mileage incrementally at only ten per cent each week to avoid risk of injury.

3. B The tried and tested method of training elite soldiers has always been through a progressive strength-training programme which consists primarily of bodyweight exercises. Push-ups, sit-ups, air squats (fingers on temples, elbows touching knees on down movement) and pull-ups should form the core foundation of the training programme.

4. A The best way to ensure you reach your fitness goals is to make sure you formulate a balanced workout plan which is integrated with plenty of rest, recovery and mobility. There are various ways to ensure this is progressive, such as increasing reps or gradually integrating new exercises into a circuit. Using a backpack filled with water bottles is a good way to progress your body-weight strength training without having to go to a gym. Start with one 500ml bottle and add a maximum of ten per cent of the weight each week.

5. C Developing strong abs is an important aspect of achieving a strong core but it needs to be paired with a strong lower back. To achieve functional fitness a strong core is essential, especially when you need to lift heavy stuff, twist, jump, grapple during sports or self defence, bend and carry out general day-to-day movements.

Photo: Official Antarctica Marathon, Richard Donavan

Jordan crossing the finish line in Antarctica

TAKE THE TEST

FIRST AID IN FREEZING WEATHER

Think you would know how to respond to an emergency in bitterly cold conditions? Let **Army Cadets National Ambassador Jordan Wylie MBE** put your first-aid knowledge to the test.

Army Cadets National Ambassador Jordan is a bestselling author, extreme adventurer, former soldier and one of the stars of Channel 4's BAFTA-nominated shows *Hunted* and *Celebrity Hunted*.

In 2018, he completed a challenge called Running Dangerously which raised more than £35,000 for charity and saw him return to three conflict zones (Iraq, Somalia and Afghanistan) where he had either served as a soldier or worked as a private military contractor. He ran marathons in each country.

Building on this incredible feat, in 2020 he started a new challenge called Running Dangerously Polar Edition in which he set out to run marathons in each of the ten coldest countries on the planet in aid of the charity Frontline Children. Read all about his cold-weather adventures then turn the page to take the first-aid test.

152   To Inspire To Achieve

» How did the Running Dangerously Polar Edition go?

I ran in Siberia, Antarctica, Greenland, Lapland, Iceland, Yukon in Canada, Svalbard in Norway, Outer Mongolia, and Alaska in the US (although the latter got terminated after 10 miles due to an avalanche warning).

Due to the global pandemic, the ongoing conflict between Russia and Ukraine and climate change challenges, I have not been able to get to the North Pole. I have now decided to reduce my carbon footprint and look for challenges that are more eco friendly.

» Why did you want to do it?

It's always about the adventure! I don't worry about times or records when running; I focus on enjoying it and being present. I often stop during the event to admire the landscape, the animals and the wilderness because I just want to enjoy the challenge, regardless of how difficult the conditions may be.

» What do you enjoy about running in the extreme cold?

The invigorating feeling of cold air on the skin, the sense of accomplishment from pushing through the elements, being immersed in the great outdoors and the opportunity to experience the most epic snowy and icy landscapes.

» What's least enjoyable?

The discomfort of being cold, the potential for frostbite or hypothermia, and the increased risk of injury on slippery surfaces.

» How do you prepare to run in freezing conditions?

It's important to properly prepare for cold-weather running by dressing in layers and learning to regulate your body temperature, wearing appropriate gear and keeping an eye on the weather forecast to ensure your safety – which should always be your main priority.

» How do you keep upbeat during a marathon?

It's about having a sense of gratitude wherever I go. I don't come from a wealthy family, nor do I earn lots of money, so I see every adventure as a great privilege. I often drift into thought when I'm running. When things get really tough, I think about friends, family and loved ones who are no longer with us and what they would do to take a few more breaths or to live a little longer.

» Why is gratitude important?

It can improve mental and physical health, increase resilience and enhance social relationships. Expressing gratitude can increase feelings of happiness, reduce stress, anxiety and depression, and increase overall life satisfaction.

Gratitude helps me foster a more positive outlook on life, helping me focus on what I have, rather than what I lack. I know I'm super lucky to travel the world on a monthly basis, so I never take it for granted.

» Advice for new runners?

Start slowly and build up gradually, invest in a good pair of running trainers and set realistic goals.

Pay attention to how your body feels when you run so you are mindful of any pain or discomfort. That's really important to help you avoid injury. Mix it up and keep things interesting by running in different locations or incorporating other types of exercise into your routine. Remember, running should be enjoyable and safe so don't put too much pressure on yourself – have fun!

» What's the best way to stay motivated when starting running?

Setting realistic goals will give you something to work towards and motivate you to keep going. Find a fellow cadet, friend or family member who also wants to take up running. This will make the experience more enjoyable and you'll have someone who will hold you accountable – and you can do the same for them.

Jordan in Iceland

'Prepare by dressing in layers and learning to regulate your body temperature'

Photo: Stephen McGrath Photography

Jordan's cold-weather adventure kit

TEST

1 You've been hiking across snow in freezing conditions when one of your group feels unwell. Which of the following signs might indicate they are suffering from hypothermia?

A. They're shivering and their skin looks pale and dry.

B. They are warm and flushed.

C. They have a full or bounding pulse.

2 If they are showing signs of hypothermia, which of these actions should you take?

A. Encourage them to lie on the ground and then raise (and support) their legs.

B. Take them indoors if possible and cover any wet clothing with a warm blanket.

C. Take them indoors if possible, protect them from the cold ground and replace any wet clothing with dry clothing.

3 If a running companion complains of the following symptoms, what would you suspect? Dry mouth, headache, feeling lightheaded and urine that is darker than usual.

A. Asthma.

B. Hypothermia.

C. Dehydration.

4 You are taking part in a training exercise and one of your group slips on ice and sustains an open fracture to their leg. As a general rule, which of these should you *not* do?

A. Give the casualty water and high-energy food.

B. Cover the wound with a double layer of sterile dressings or clean padding and secure it with a bandage.

C. Immobilise the injured body part and arrange to transport the casualty to hospital.

Jordan running with reindeer

Photo: Stephen McGrath Photography

5 **Your group have been sheltering from the wind in freezing conditions. One of your party complains of pins and needles in their feet and thinks they might have frostbite. What is it?**

A. A condition that occurs after a tick has bitten a person and become frozen beneath their skin.

B. When the tissues of the extremities – usually the fingers and toes – freeze due to low temperatures.

C. Stiffening of the ankle joint due to extreme cold weather.

ANSWERS

1. A With hypothermia (when the body temperature falls below 35C), the blood supply to the superficial blood vessels in the skin shuts down to maintain the function of vital organs (such as the heart and brain) so shivering and pale, dry skin are key signs to look out for. Your fellow hiker may also have a slow pulse and their breathing could be slow and shallow.

2. C You should take the person with hypothermia to a sheltered place as quickly as possible and protect them from the cold ground. Remove and replace any wet clothing if possible, then dial 999 or 112 for help. Warm them by giving them warm drinks and high-energy foods, such as chocolate, while continuing to monitor their vital signs.

3. C Dehydration occurs when the amount of fluids lost from the body is not replaced adequately. This may lead to a dry mouth and dry eyes and cause headaches, dizziness, confusion, cramp and urine that's dark in colour.

4. A With any fracture as a rule you should not give the casualty any food or drink because an anaesthetic might be needed.

Other things to avoid are moving the casualty before the injured part is secured and supported (unless they are in immediate danger) and, in the case of an open fracture, pressing directly on a protruding bone end.

5. B Frostbite occurs when the body's extremities freeze in low temperatures. It usually occurs in freezing or cold and windy conditions. People who cannot move around to increase their circulation are particularly susceptible.

Another sign of frostbite might be a change in the colour of their skin (first white and then mottled and blue). It can also be accompanied by hypothermia.

Army Cadet Yearbook Issue 4

TAKE THE TEST
ANNUAL CAMP

Lt Col Mike Doyle, Deputy Commandant, Middlesex and North West London ACF, puts your knowledge of this annual highlight to the test.

» Why is annual camp so significant in the Army Cadets calendar?

Annual camp is something cadets work towards throughout the entire year and is a culmination of their training. The syllabus is broken down into star grades and, as long as they attend everything throughout the training year, cadets should pass their next star badge at the end of annual camp.

Camp is the only time in the year when the whole County lives and trains together for an extended period, so it's also a time to mix with friends and make new ones.

» What's the best way to prepare?

It's key to listen to instructions given by your detachment commander. They will brief you on what you will be doing at camp and provide a kit list. Even at the same annual camp not every cadet will be doing the same thing, so you need to make sure you have everything you need for the activities you'll be involved in.

To go to camp you'll need to pass your basic training test and have spent a weekend away with Army Cadets. That weekend separated from your family will help you get used to being away from home; annual camp may last one or two weeks and we don't want cadets to get really homesick during that time.

Leicestershire, Northamptonshire and Rutland ACF annual camp 2021

Glasgow and Lanarkshire ACF at Strensall 2022

Photo Kate Knight

TAKE THE TEST

'Most cadets go home with a huge group of new friends because they have bonded during activities'

» Advice for nervous first-timers?

Have a chat with one or two senior cadets before you go. We get a lot of cadets who are nervous about attending annual camp for the first time, yet almost all come back declaring it one of the best experiences they've ever had. Give it a chance by talking to others who've been before and know what it's like.

» What if cadets fear they'll be out of their depth in the activities?

It's natural to feel apprehensive before you go away for the first time, but be reassured that the training you do will be pitched at your level. We won't expect you to be Rambo! For instance, if you're asked to sleep out in the field for a couple of nights, you won't be left on your own or left to the elements. Experienced instructors will be looking after you.

» How can cadets get the most out of annual camp?

Some cadets might feel apprehensive about a particular activity, but the advice is to get stuck in and give it a go. Often cadets find that once they give an activity a try, they enjoy taking part and usually go home with lots of fun stories.

» How should cadets cope with feeling homesick?

One of the best ways to deal with feeling homesick is to phone home. There is time built into the itinerary for cadets to ring their parents or guardians. If they don't have access to a phone, an instructor will be able to set them up with one.

Cadets experiencing homesickness can also talk to friends, senior cadets and instructors. There is also a padre at annual camp who is there to support cadets with all welfare concerns and will be happy to talk about anything they might be experiencing.

Army Cadet Yearbook Issue 4   157

2nd Battalion Highlanders annual camp 2022

Crowborough Camp 2023

» What personal attributes do cadets gain at annual camp?

At all levels of the syllabus cadets learn self-reliance. To follow their camp programme they need to be something of a self-starter and be prepared for all of their activities.

They'll also learn to work as part of a team. Most cadets go home with a huge group of new friends – even best friends – because they have worked together on tasks and bonded during activities and downtime.

Everyone also gains some kind of leadership experience, which ranges from senior cadets doing their 4-Star fieldcraft to a cadet on their first annual camp who takes responsibility for a domestic job.

» Final word of advice for cadets and CFAVs attending annual camp?

Even if they've been heavily briefed beforehand, they should be prepared for it all to be thrown out of the window. For example, they might lose a training area they had booked and be faced with a plan B. If cadets and CFAVs can go with the flow in every situation and enjoy it for what it is, they'll have the best time.

TEST

1 How many people attended Army Cadets annual camps in 2022?

A. 28,880.

B. 14,880.

C. 7,880.

2 When was the first annual camp held?

A. 1909.

B. 1989.

C. 1889.

3 What must a cadet have achieved to attend their first annual camp?

A. Have a 50 per cent attendance record at their detachment over a period of 12 months and have successfully spent a weekend away from home with Army Cadets.

B. Have passed APC 2-Star and successfully spent a training weekend away from home with Army Cadets.

C. Passed a basic training test and successfully spent a training weekend away from home with Army Cadets.

TAKE THE TEST

4. Is there financial aid available if a cadet's family struggles to cover the costs of attending annual camp?

A. No.

B. Yes.

C. It depends where in the UK they live.

5. Where are annual camps held?

A. Always at military bases in the UK.

B. Mostly at military bases in the UK.

C. Always at military bases abroad.

ANSWERS

1. A Annual camp is a hugely popular highlight in the Army Cadets calendar and in 2022 a whopping 28,880 people attended camps in the UK. There were 6,654 attendees from CCF Army Cadets at CTT camps, 3,228 attendees at CCF-run camps and 18,998 attendees at ACF camps.

2. C To take part in an annual camp is to take part in a very long tradition. Camps are nearly as old as the Cadet Force and the first record of a camp taking place was in 1889 at Churn Downs in Oxfordshire.

3. C To be permitted to attend their first annual camp, a cadet must have passed the recruit's ACF basic training test and have successfully spent at least one training weekend away from home with Army Cadets.

4. B Annual camps have a charge attached to them. This mostly covers the cost of food and external activities such as Adventurous Training. It is generally lower than the kind of costs charged in other youth organisations (and much lower than if you did the same activities commercially).

A cadet should not be prevented from attending annual camp because their family struggles to pay the cost. There are many exemptions, funds and grants available to ensure everyone can receive the full Cadets experience. Cadets who wish to attend annual camp, or any other activity, but who can't afford it should let their instructors know as soon as possible so they can put a plan into action.

5. B Annual camps are mostly held at military bases in the UK, although in the past cadets have attended camps in Germany and Cyprus.

Photo: Kate Knight

2nd Battalion The Highlanders ACF camp

Photos: Kate Knight

TAKE THE TEST
NAVIGATION

Are you a whizz with a map and compass? Let **National Navigation Officer Colonel William "Ginge" Morris** put your orienteering skills to the test.

A penchant for planning routes, taking bearings, reading maps and mastering a compass began for Colonel William "Ginge" Morris ACF when he joined the Cadets in 1976.

Ginge first learned to use a map and compass when he undertook his Bronze Duke of Edinburgh (DofE) Award. He then went on to complete Gold and, after leaving Army Cadets in 1980, joined the Army where he utilised his orienteering skills. Today, he advises CFAVs who want to teach navigation skills to budding adventurers within Army Cadets.

As Commandant of Gwent and Powys ACF, he also enjoys seeing cadets take the Army Proficiency Certificate and progress from one star to four star in their navigation skills.

» What's the best advice you have ever been given about navigation?

When I was a cadet doing my Bronze DofE at Crowborough Training Camp in Sussex, I had a great instructor, Captain Byron Jenkins, who told me that a map is like a big storyboard. If you spend all your time looking at the storyboard rather than the real-life picture in front of you, then you'll get confused and lost.

To this day, I tell my trainees the same thing: think of your map as your storyboard and, once you've confirmed where you are, then start observing the greatest source of information which is the ground beneath you and the terrain over which you'll be walking. You then only need to refer to your map for tick off points (for instance an upcoming turning) along the way.

'Know where you want to go, but never forget where you came from'

» Are we all capable of being able to navigate?

Everyone, from parents to children and pets, has a sense of navigation. When a new cadet is scared of navigation we ask them to draw where they live and their local school on a piece of paper. We then ask them to map out how they usually get to their school: which way they turn on leaving their house, the roads they take and any tick off points (for instance a local shop or a football field) along the way.

» Other than a map and compass, what do you need for navigation?

In training, we ask a person where they want to go and to write down on a route card how they would get there. We ask other participants if they understand the destination and the route they would need to take to get there. We then say: *'Okay, you take us there.'* They often look at us as if to say: *'How are we going to do that?'* We remind them they have their route card with all the directions and tick off points. Then they're happy to lead the way without their face being constantly buried in their map and compass.

» What leadership qualities do you develop by mastering navigation?

Confidence and self-reliance are key attributes but also the ability to plan and prepare. When you're taking part in navigation you're likely to be out for several hours so you need to think ahead about what equipment to take, what clothing you will require and what food and water provisions you will need. You'll also need to prepare a route card in advance and leave a copy with a responsible person so that, if you're not back by an agreed time, they will know where to look for you.

» Why is map reading such a useful tool?

It's a core skill embedded in many disciplines within the Army Cadets syllabus. For example, if you are doing fieldcraft and told by your company commander to find an enemy position, or meet someone at a rendezvous point, you would need to get there using a map and compass.

A cadet doing the DofE Award may be exceptionally fit and motivated but would fail if they couldn't navigate to checkpoints. In first aid, you need to be able to pinpoint your location on a map and communicate the correct grid references to emergency services if you need to call for help while on expedition. Even within shooting, arcs of fire are measured using compass bearings so that firing stays within a safety zone.

» What are the most common difficulties with navigation?

Some struggle with the mathematics needed to do what we call a 'back bearing', but there are tips to overcome this. Others become confused about which arrow to follow on their compass: the arrow direction or the magnetic needle? The magnetic needle moves around so it always points north, therefore it's important not to accidentally follow it and head off in the wrong direction.

» What's your favourite piece of life advice?

Always know where you want to go but never forget where you came from. If something goes wrong, you can always retreat to where you came from.

TAKE THE TEST

1 Which of these symbols correctly matches its description?

A. Current or former place of worship with a spire.

B. Underground station.

C. Hospital.

2 What are the lines on a map called that indicate the height of ground?

A. Contour lines.
B. Composition lines.
C. Curve lines.

3 What is the name of the numbers on a map, that increase as you go left to right?

A. Northings.
B. Eastings.
C. Southings.

4 What are the three common norths we use in navigation?

A Magnetic north, grid north, true north.
B Magnetic north, grid north, polar north.
C Magnetic north, geographic north, true north.

5 Can you work out the six-figure grid reference for A, B and C in the example below?

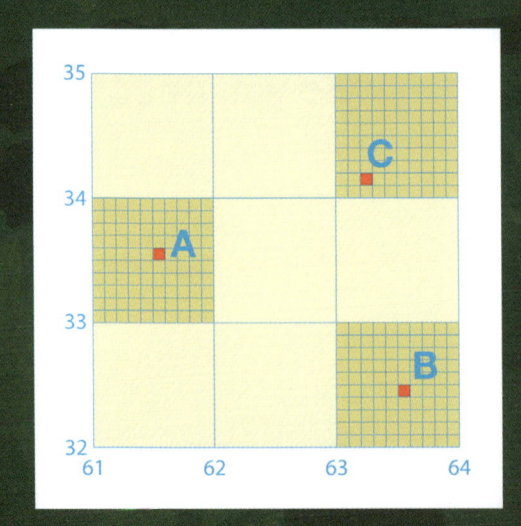

ANSWERS

1. A

This sign indicates a current or former place of worship that has a spire, so is the correct answer.

This sign indicates a bus or coach station, not an underground station.

This sign indicates a heliport not a hospital.

Maps have symbols to represent different landmarks such as places of worship, car parks, pubs and schools. You can match symbols with the corresponding landmarks in your surroundings to help locate your position on the map. Each map will have a key to its symbols so, if in doubt about the meaning of a symbol, consult the key.

2. A The height and shape of the land is shown on a map using contour lines. These are thin orange or brown lines with numbers on them. The number tells you the height above sea level of that line. A contour line is drawn between points of equal height, so any single contour line will be at the same height all the way along its length. The map key will tell you the contour interval used.

3. B Before you begin to look at grid references it is important to be aware that all the numbers going across the face of the map, for example, left to right, are called eastings (this is because they are heading eastward). Similarly, all the numbers going up the face of the map from bottom to top are called northings (because they head in a northward direction).

4. A Magnetic north – the direction any magnet compass will point.

Grid north – the direction of a vertical (north-south) grid line on an OS map.

True north – the direction to the Earth's geographic north pole.

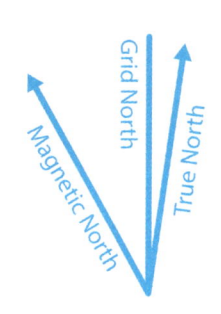

5. A 615 335 **B** 635 324 **C** 632 341

When giving a four-figure grid reference you give the eastings number first and the northings number second – you go along the corridor (horizontal) and then up the stairs (vertical). This will give you the basic four-figure grid reference.

For example, the four-figure grid reference for point A is 61- 33 -.

To get the six-figure grid reference, imagine this square is divided up with 10 squares along each side. Still remembering to go along the corridor and up the stairs, work out the extra numbers you need and put them into your four-figure grid reference.

For example, the six-figure grid reference for point A is 615 335.

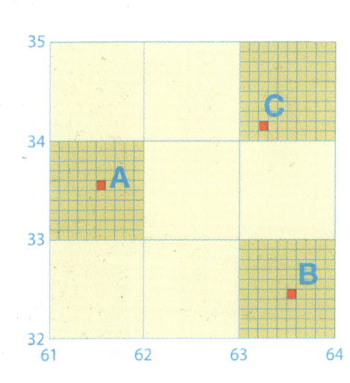

LEADERSHIP

Want the lowdown on how to master leadership skills? We aked three experts, who've demonstrated leadership in challenging real-life situations, to share what they've learnt from experience.

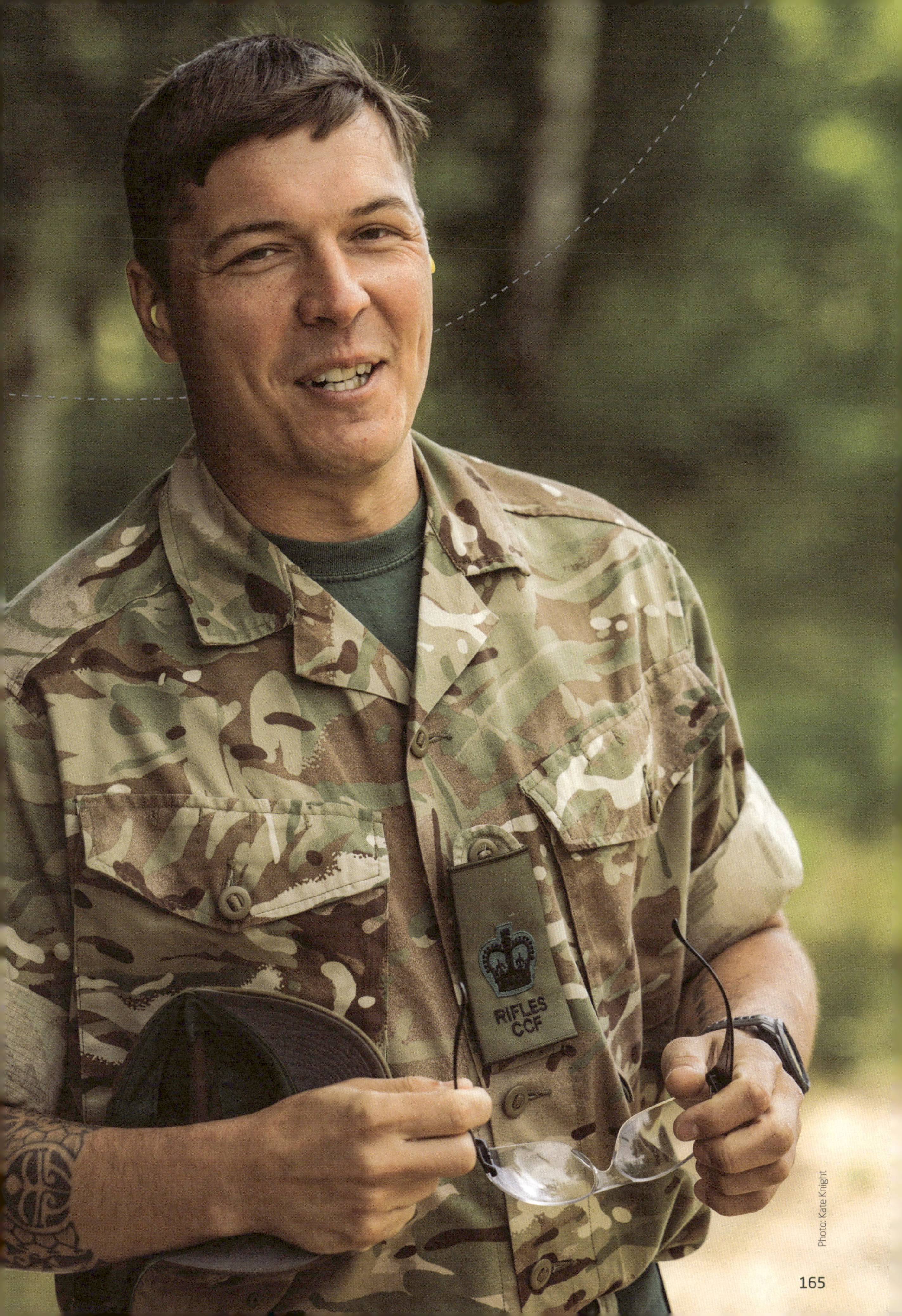

Photo: Kate Knight

REACH for the SKY

Mandy with a Tornado GR4 aircraft

Photo: Dan Tidswell

Fighter pilot **Mandy Hickson** reveals how cadets can learn to take their leadership skills stratospheric.

A pioneering spirit, mental resilience and outstanding bravery characterise fighter pilot Mandy Hickson and her trailblazing career.

One of the first female cadets in the Air Training Corps, in 1998 Mandy went on to become the second female RAF pilot to fly the Tornado GR4, and completed three tours of duty – and 45 missions – over Iraq.

Today the groundbreaking pilot is a motivational speaker and author, and enjoys nothing more than sharing her unique frontline experiences and revealing the crucial lessons they taught her about leadership. Read on to discover Mandy's top tips for cadets with ambitions to become first-rate leaders.

> *'I was resilient, determined and passionate about becoming a pilot so I kept going'*

Above: Beside a Hawk training aircraft in 1998

» Recognise and develop potential

From a young age, I wanted to be a pilot like my grandfather. In 1986, I joined the Air Training Corps the first night it opened its doors to girls. Later, I joined my university's air squadron and began to work towards a career in the RAF but, despite my best efforts, I kept failing the computerised flying tests.

Fortunately, my squadron boss had a leadership style that boosted my confidence rather than undermining it. He believed in my flying ability and argued for a formal review of the testing system. He was right: it was found to be biased against women. Rather than distance himself from me and focus on my failings, he chose to become an ally and focused on advocating for my strengths – even when I was in the minority and the odds were stacked against me.

It's completely normal to fail sometimes when you're learning new things and breaking barriers. You become more resilient as a result, but it takes time. A good leader recognises the differing needs, abilities and resilience levels of those in their team and helps each member achieve their potential, which allows the whole team to achieve its goals.

» Words are powerful, so choose them carefully

Initially, I had to join the RAF as an air traffic controller, but I was eventually given the chance to train as a pilot. The leadership team at the time told me I was a test case and they wanted to see how far a female pilot would get before failing. Their choice of words had a massive effect on me; I was being given the chance of a lifetime, but it was phrased as a countdown to failure. As a result, every time I was met with a challenge – and there were many – I wondered whether this was going to be the point at which I failed.

Each time I succeeded, it heightened the feeling of imposter syndrome and, instead of celebrating being one step closer to success, I continually felt I was in some way closer to failure. However, I was resilient, determined and passionate about becoming a pilot so I kept going. Although the rest of my squadron were men, they were supportive and made me feel part of the team rather than just a test case.

The experience taught me the importance of effective communication within a team, especially when you're in a leadership role. It can make a big difference to the morale and motivation of your team members.

'Although the military has ranks, missions aren't always led by the highest-ranking officer'

Above: Mandy as one of the first female cadets in the Air Training Corps

Right: Mandy (third row) pictured with II (AC) Squadron in Iraq in 2000

Photo: Crown Copyright 2000

Photo: Dan Tidswell

» Be true to yourself and support others to do the same

Eventually, I worked my way into the seat of the Tornado GR4 fast jet, but the challenges kept coming! Over the years, I experienced practical challenges, like not having women's toilets in buildings and there being no flying suits for women, which involved lots of letter writing and campaigning for change. Others were more cultural, like expectations about my behaviour. I found myself morphing into being 'one of the lads' in a bid to fit in, but at times I was also expected to behave 'like a lady'. Finding my place was very challenging.

I experienced bullying at one stage in my career. It wasn't until much later, with the support of my partner, that I felt able to speak to the person about how their actions made me feel. Facing challenges alone or trying to instigate change can be intimidating. Sometimes it can feel easier and safer to just go with the flow, especially if you don't feel able to talk to those in authority. But I've learnt that good leaders do listen when you confide in them and that change is possible, so it's worth being brave, speaking up and, most importantly, staying true to yourself.

» Share leadership

A positive leader understands that a team can be strengthened by encouraging team members to embrace and share their individuality, which can be informed by gender, background and cognitive differences. Diversity and equality in a team are important strengths. Although the military has ranks, missions aren't always led by the highest-ranking officer, so a key part of everyone's training is to develop teamwork and leadership skills.

When I was a junior pilot serving in Iraq, I was leading a formation that was engaged by a missile. Despite the complexity of the mission spiralling, my boss didn't take over. We were all trained in **DODAR** decision making: **D**iagnosing the issue, **O**ptions analysis, **D**eciding on the course of action, **A**ssigning tasks and, if necessary, **R**eviewing the situation. It enabled us to react quickly under pressure, no matter who was leading the formation.

It demonstrated the importance of empowering the whole team, so any team member could lead and all of them could work effectively with the appointed leader. I'd also encourage any team member to step up if you're given a leadership opportunity. It's only by pushing yourself out of your comfort zone that you discover who you are and what you enjoy.

Above: in the University of Birmingham Air Squadron

❱❱ Recognise the responsibility of being a role model

I think the word 'leader' describes what someone does, rather than who they are. I've never really seen myself as a leader and I haven't had lots of stereotypical leadership roles in my career but, more recently, I realised that others have been following my lead.

I'd taken a cadet for a flight experience and she was very sullen and withdrawn throughout the flight, but was clearly an excellent young pilot. When I asked why she was so quiet, she told me she hadn't wanted to throw her whole self into the experience in case she failed. When I told her what an incredible pilot she was, she didn't believe me at first but, gradually, her face lit up. I saw her again a year later when she was taking her pilot exams. She said she wanted to become a pilot just like me. Her words really struck me. I realised how much fear holds us down yet confidence lifts us up.

What could we achieve if we weren't afraid of failure? I had started to train to be an airline pilot because that's what lots of ex-military pilots do. Just as I'd done my whole life, I was trying to fit in again. I was afraid of being seen as different but, in a moment of reflection, I realised that my difference is my strength. Instead of becoming an airline pilot, I decided to be brave and set up my own motivational speaking business and share my experience to inspire and empower others.

Role models take many forms and so do leaders. I still have imposter syndrome but, when I receive emails from people telling me I've been a role model to them, I realise the true power of positive leadership: it's not what you achieve, it's what you enable others to achieve.

Go further

Mandy's book *An Officer, Not A Gentleman* is available to buy from bookshops.

Scan the QR code to watch her talk about her experiences on the frontline and what she learnt about herself.

12 TIPS FOR AUTHENTIC LEADERSHIP

Sarah McEntee, SO2 Leadership Cadet Forces, thinks we've all got the capability to be an authentic leader – if we understand what it takes.

There are thousands of books written about leadership, thousands more videos online and numerous gurus waiting to turn you into an inspiring leader. Bad leadership leads to disasters while good leadership is probably the single way people can change the world for the better.

Does leadership take years of practice? Hours reading academic books? Do you need an important-sounding job title? Actually, no! In 1952, the great military leader Field Marshal Slim spoke to a group of officer cadets at Royal Military Academy Sandhurst and said: *'Leadership is the most personal thing in the world, for the simple reason that leadership is just plain you'.*

Read on to discover 12 insights that'll help you develop authentic leadership skills.

1 Know yourself

Trying to be someone you are not might work for a while but, over time, will become exhausting.

The first thing every leader must understand is themselves: their strengths and weaknesses, how to make the most of the things they're great at, and what they can do to develop in areas that are challenging.

Don't be afraid to accept there are some things you simply won't excel at as a leader; that's where having a great team comes in. Take time to discover who you are and which leadership style feels most comfortable and intuitive to you. A good starting point might be taking the personality quiz in the Go Further box at the end of this feature.

'The single most important thing is to lead authentically'

2. Know your people

Why does that cadet in your detachment always turn up late and in the incorrect uniform? Why has a previously brilliant cadet suddenly decided to leave? Why has your second in command decided not to talk to you this evening?

To be a supportive leader, as well as a leader who can challenge when required, you need to have a good understanding of the people in your team.

Colonel Neil Jurd OBE is the Director of Initial Officer Training for the ACF and in *The Leadership Book* he talks about The Foundations Model (Figure A).

On the surface we see a person's behaviour, achievements, performance and focus, but all those things are impacted by what is going on underneath at foundation level. These are things we can't see but as leaders we need to understand. What might be going on beneath the surface for the people described above?

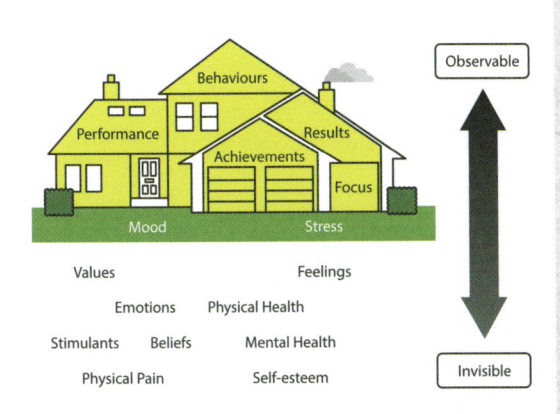

3. Communication matters

Can you think of a time when something didn't go to plan? Chances are poor communication played a large part in messing up that plan. One of my favourite leadership concepts is the Communications Pyramid, because it's a simple, relatable and easy-to-use leadership tool (Figure B, over the page).

Below the bottom of the pyramid is the dreaded Tomb; where there is no connection, no communication, nothing. This is the person you walk by every day to catch the bus and don't even acknowledge each other. In fact, you actively choose to avoid them by looking down or away. You probably do this many times a day.

4. Ritual and Cliché

Level one is the domain of Ritual and Cliché conversations. Where I live in the northwest of the UK, most mornings I see the same people and we say, *'Hi, you alright'?* The reply is: *'Yeah I'm alright'*. We've spoken but it's a ritual. It's the same thing every morning and the answer is almost unimportant.

Figure A The Foundations Model from *The Leadership Book* by Neil Jurd OBE

5 Facts and Information

At Level two is Facts and Information. This is the sharing zone, where we discuss things we know or have heard. On detachment night, these might be the chats you have with cadets about kit or perhaps you're passing on instructions about the plans for the night. Some cases, like issuing a set of orders, are essential information. As a leader you'll often have conversations at this level, but it isn't where you really get to know people.

6 Ideas and Judgements

Personalities and ideas begin to shine through when you reach the level of Ideas and Judgements. You might begin to get this towards the end of a training session or perhaps by day two or three of an overnight exercise on annual camp. It's where people begin to share their opinions. As a leader you want to encourage this level of communication, particularly when you are relying on a team to work together to find a solution on a cold, dark and windy night in the middle of a training area.

7 Emotions and Feelings

The magic really begins to happen at level four: Emotions and Feelings. This is the type of conversation where you get to know the team you're leading. You build trust and can have open and honest conversations on an emotional level. You might have experienced this with your best mates or maybe towards the end of a camp or course. It is where, as a leader, you should aspire to be with your team.

8 Peak level

Beyond level four is Peak: when you don't need to say anything to your team as a look or a nod is enough to inspire an action. It's a pretty cool place to be and is probably where you are with your very best friends. So how do you progress from Ritual and Cliché, or even worse the Tomb, to Feelings and Emotions and Peak? In the Army Cadets we can find ourselves in many exciting and challenging situations where we must build relationships with new people quite quickly.

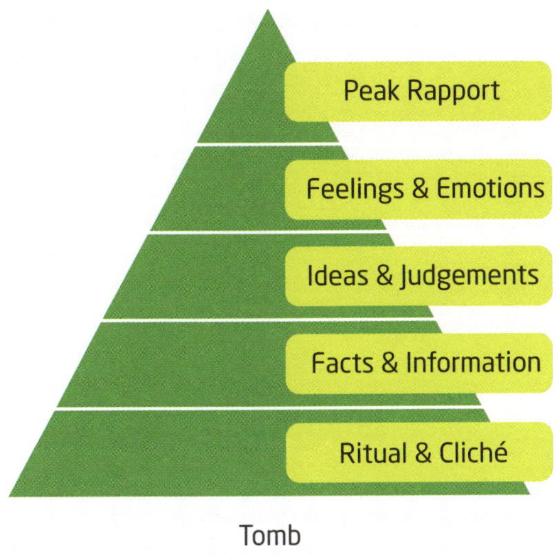
Peak Rapport
Feelings & Emotions
Ideas & Judgements
Facts & Information
Ritual & Cliché
Tomb

Figure B The Communications Pyramid by Father John Powell

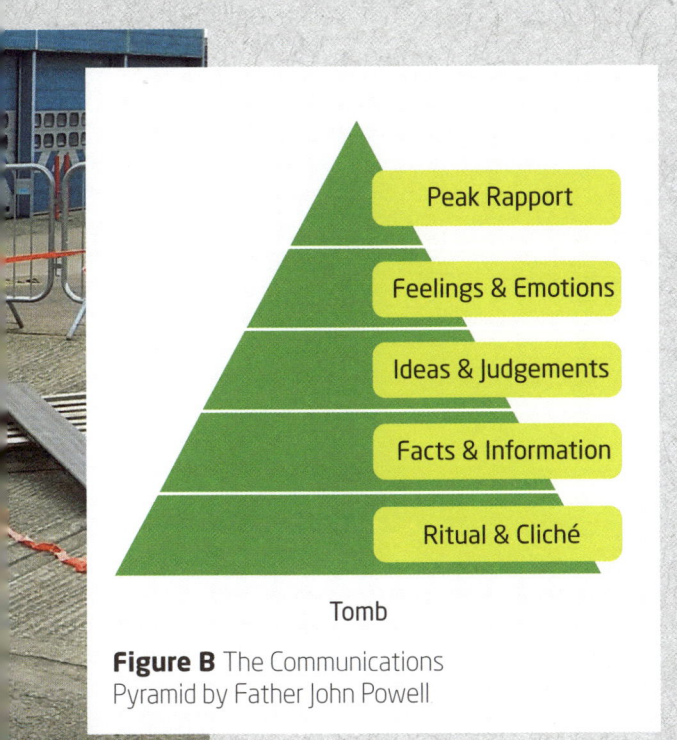

'The magic really begins to happen at level four'

9 Build rapport

Before I had the privilege of working for the Army Cadets, I spent many years as a radio presenter. My first job was to drive around and call back into the morning show with live, often silly, links. I spent one morning broadcasting from inside a metal dustbin on a golf driving range.

In every scenario I had a very limited amount of time to brief members of the public on what to say (Facts and Information in Figure B above) and in every case I had to very quickly build rapport, calm their nerves and lead them through something out of their comfort zone (Feelings and Emotions in Figure B above). At the same time I needed to have a deep understanding of what the guys in the studio wanted, which frequently changed at the last minute. I had to be at Peak level with my co-hosts.

How did I do it? When I turned up, I tried to build a rapport by asking questions to find common ground. Sometimes that might simply be saying I was feeling nervous too and that we'd get through the moment together and enjoy it. By being honest about my feelings and emotions in that moment, I was able to move quickly from level two to level four of the pyramid in Figure B.

10 Take risks

In your role as leader, you could be dropped into a team and have very little time to build connection. It can be challenging to start conversations that move you up the pyramid. It feels risky, but my best advice is to spend time listening before talking. Look for the unseen (body language) and know that by sharing your feelings you're allowing others to share theirs. That's how you get people on board and what enables a leader to support when needed and challenge when required.

11 Communicate your vision

One of the three core components of the Army Cadet Leadership Code is 'vision'. You can have all the leadership skills in the world but if you and your team don't know what the purpose or mission is, everything becomes unfocused and people lose interest.

Elon Musk's SpaceX company has a strong, clear and compelling vision: *'To revolutionise space technology with the ultimate goal of enabling people to live on other planets'.* Sports brand Nike uses: *'Nike strives to support every athlete in the world'.* That includes you and me, not just Sir Mo Farah!

Whether you are leading the same team every week in your detachment, or are assigned a team as part of a single exercise, you'll need to know what your vision is and how to communicate it clearly.

12 Learn from mistakes

Leadership can be challenging and sometimes lonely. Leadership in the Army Cadets frequently requires you to step up and lead your friendship group, which can also change those relationships. You won't always get things right, but accepting failure and learning from it is something great leaders embrace. Your leadership style will evolve and develop over the years, but the single most important thing you can do is to lead authentically. After all, *'leadership is just plain you'.*

Go further

Scan the QR code to take a personality test and discover more about your leadership style.

SALLY ORANGE'S 7 WAYS TO BE MORE RESILIENT

Photo: World Marathon Challenge

Sally at the finishing line in Antarctica

In January 2023, **Army Cadets National Ambassador Sally Orange** completed seven marathons on seven continents in seven days. We asked her to share seven lessons she learnt about resilience while undertaking this extraordinary challenge.

Being resilient (having the ability to cope with and bounce back from adversity) is an essential life skill which all cadets should develop. It's also an important characteristic of a good leader.

Sally Orange, ex-servicewoman, adventure athlete and mental-health campaigner, knows how crucial it is to be resilient enough to go through a difficult experience and come out the other side. In February, she undertook a mammoth marathon challenge and, in the process, learnt some important lessons about mental and physical resilience.

In an epic running endeavour, she undertook seven marathons in seven days on seven continents (Antarctica, Africa, Australasia, Asia, Europe, South America and North America).

Despite some very low moments, Sally succeeded in completing the World Marathon Challenge and is the first female veteran – and only the fifth British woman – to have done so. It was incredibly gruelling but Sally persevered by calling upon her inner resources and strength, which is something she believes we can all learn to do. We asked her to share some of the things she learnt during the experience and to reveal a few tips that helped her when the going got tough.

1. Reframe the experience

Experience: I was in Spain (five marathons into the event, miles from home and far away from friends and family) when I got an upset stomach. I felt so ill I was crying while running; it was a horrible experience, both mentally and physically.

Insight: I had previously listened to a podcast about a woman paralysed from the neck down, who wished she could go for a walk with her mum. So instead of being upset about not being able to run the marathon at that stage, I made myself appreciate just being able to walk.

Tip: Instead of being annoyed because you don't feel able to do what you want to do, try focusing on what you can do to continue your journey towards your goal – even if you have to delay reaching it.

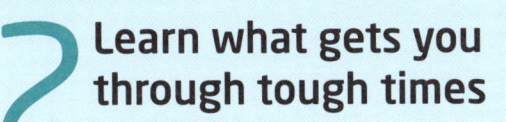

2. Learn what gets you through tough times

Experience: When I had the experience above, some runners stopped to ask if I needed help. I was in so much pain I couldn't think straight and didn't know how to respond. I didn't want to slow them down or put them to any trouble, so I just said 'No, thank you'.

Insight: With hindsight, I should have asked for some water. Despite all my preparation for the challenge, I didn't have a plan to deal with illness. They would have easily been able to help me if I'd known what I needed. I've learnt from that experience, so I'll be better able to communicate with people if it ever happens again.

Tip: When we feel down, ill or anxious, it's hard to know what we need to help us feel better. We can't learn to swim in a storm, so it's important to make the most of calm waters to prepare for more turbulent seas. When you're feeling well, make a list of things that make you happy and relaxed and keep it somewhere accessible like your phone. Tell people about the list, so they will know how to help you. Most people want to help – they just don't always know what to do.

Sally enjoying the support of a good friend during her marathon challenge

> **'I undertake challenges wearing fruit costumes to start a conversation about mental wellbeing'**

3. Use the power of distraction

Experience: The Dubai marathon was another low point for me. I found the event particularly difficult and relied heavily on all my resilience strategies to get me to the finish line. Halfway, I had to reframe my goal: instead of it being the finish line, it became the nearest lamppost, then the next lamppost, and so on – anything further felt impossible.

Insight: Six miles from the end, a friend met me and ran with me for a while. She was just in her flip-flops, chatting away, but the distraction, laughter and support massively boosted my morale. Dubai went from being my worst marathon to one of the most enjoyable because of my friend's support.

Tip: Sometimes, all our usual coping strategies don't seem to work. When this happens, try reaching out to a friend. Maybe do one of the things on your 'happy list' with them, like watching a film or eating your favourite food. You don't need to talk to them about how you're feeling – unless you want to. Just focus on enjoying whatever you're doing in that moment.

Sally running in Cape Town, South Africa

Photo: World Marathon Challenge

Sally's 2023 adventures

Sally completed this year's London Marathon, swam the English Channel, and took part in both an Ironman event in Estonia and the Escape from Alcatraz Triathlon in San Francisco.

Sally dressed as a pod of peas in Antarctica

4 Celebrate successes

Experience: It can take years to prepare for adventurous expeditions and endurance challenges. Before this challenge, I had lots of rejections from potential sponsors. It can be hard to stay confident and motivated when you're faced with obstacles before you even start. However, you only need one sponsor to say yes and it changes everything.

Insight: When someone agrees to sponsor me or I tick something off my to-do list – no matter how small – I try to celebrate that achievement. Then, the next time I have to face something intimidating, or on days when I don't feel I've accomplished much, I think about what I *have* achieved. It helps to lift my spirits and boost my confidence.

Tip: It can be helpful to imagine achievements as cookies in a jar. Each time you achieve something you find challenging, add it to the cookie jar. You could write the accomplishment on a piece of paper and pop it in a real cookie jar. When you need a boost, read one of your achievement cookies.

5 Break challenges into bite-size chunks

Experience: Before the World Marathon Challenge, I was diagnosed with a stress fracture in my foot, so I couldn't start the physical element of my training until six weeks before the event. It was hard not to panic and worry about letting people down.

Insight: Instead of tackling my event preparation in a fixed order, I decided to break it down into sections. I worked with a resilience coach and focused on the mental element during times when I couldn't run. I then progressed to the physical training later.

Tip: There are usually lots of ways to complete a challenge. If you don't feel physically or mentally able to complete it as you'd planned, break it down into bite-size chunks. This can help you identify which chunks are proving problematic. Then you can work out the best way, and in what order, to tackle each chunk to achieve your goal.

'Each time you achieve something challenging, add it to the cookie jar'

6 Improvise. Adapt. Overcome.

Experience: Due to an issue with the aeroplane, we had to complete the last three marathons in just 36 hours. Sleep plays a big role in my mental health and resilience. I knew this change to the timetable would impact my sleep, so I had to develop a strategy to overcome – or at least mitigate – it.

Insight: I applied the 'Improvise. Adapt. Overcome' strategy. I let go of the things I couldn't control (where and when I slept) and focused on the things I could control. Whenever and wherever I had the chance to sleep, I tried to sleep. If I couldn't sleep, I focused on resting. If I couldn't rest, I focused on relaxing. Instead of getting frustrated and anxious, I just kept improvising and adapting.

Tip: The reason you've got a 100 per cent record of surviving every day of your life so far is because you've adapted and improvised to overcome things (often without even thinking about it). When circumstances feel out of control, use this strategy to remind yourself you still have some control. You could adapt your methods of achieving your goal or you could decide to adapt the goal itself.

7 Believe in yourself

Experience: For the Antarctic marathon, I dressed as a pod of frozen peas. All the other runners were in all-weather gear with their faces covered. I looked different from them but I didn't care. I've discovered that being myself and not being afraid to stand out has benefits. I often undertake challenges while wearing fruit or veg costumes to make people smile and start a conversation about mental wellbeing.

Insight: My costume was like a beacon in the snowy landscape and made people smile. Like all my fun costumes, it was a talking point – a chance to raise awareness of mental health in a way that made people feel comfortable and able to share their own experiences.

Tip: Embrace who you are and what really matters to you. It can be hard to follow your dreams or feel confident in your own skin when people around you have different ideas and opinions. See the positives in the things that make you unique – and then try to make a positive difference in life.

Go further

Scan the QR code to find out about the seven charities Sally supported during her seven marathons and find out how to create your own 7-7-7 adventure.

LEADERSHIP

Army Cadet Yearbook Issue 4

CADET LIFE

Skill-up with exped tips from the experts, learn about CyberFirst, get the low-down on first aid and hydration, and meet the organisations making exciting AT and other opportunities a reality for more cadets.

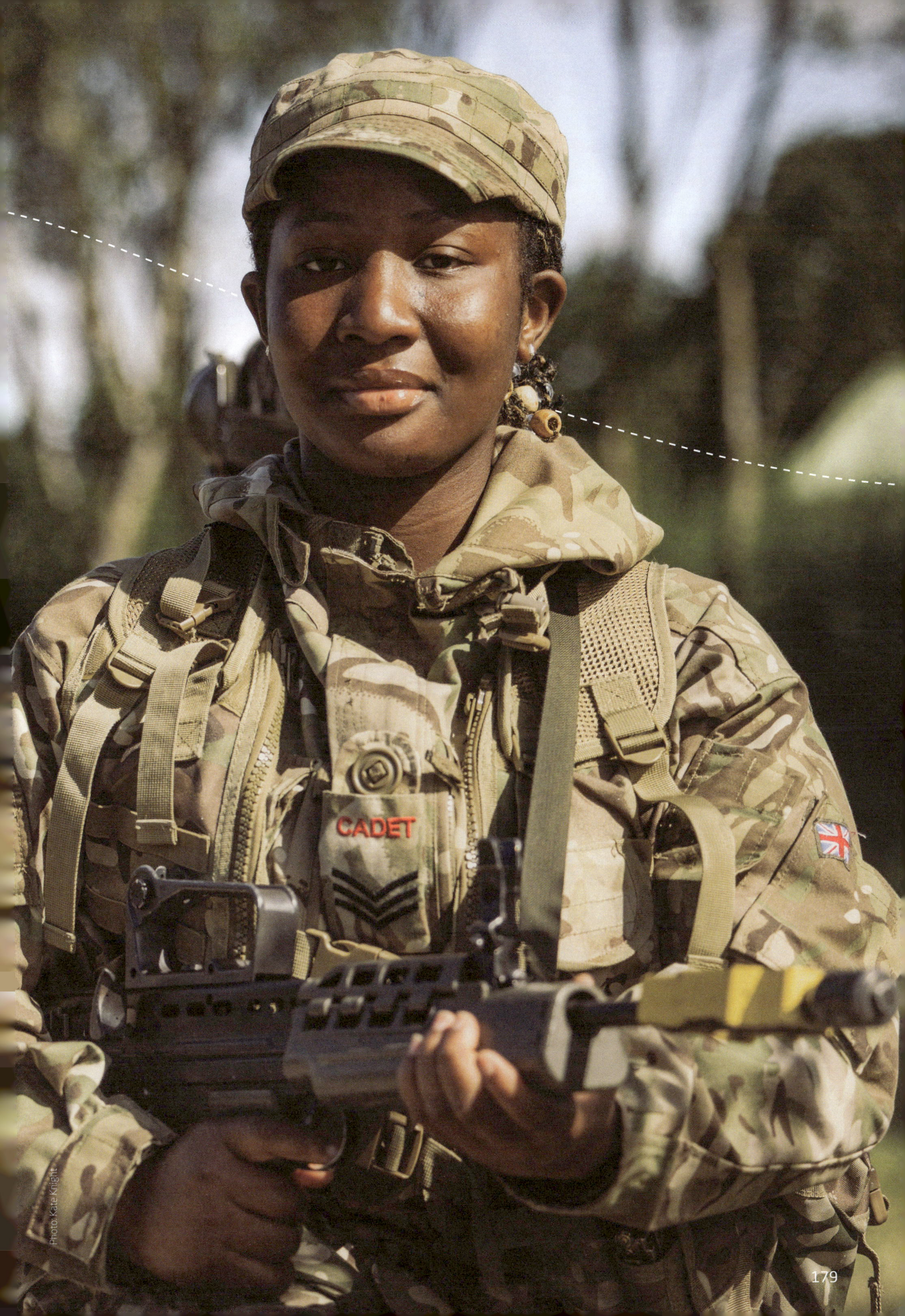

Photo: Kate Knight

TOP EXPED TIPS

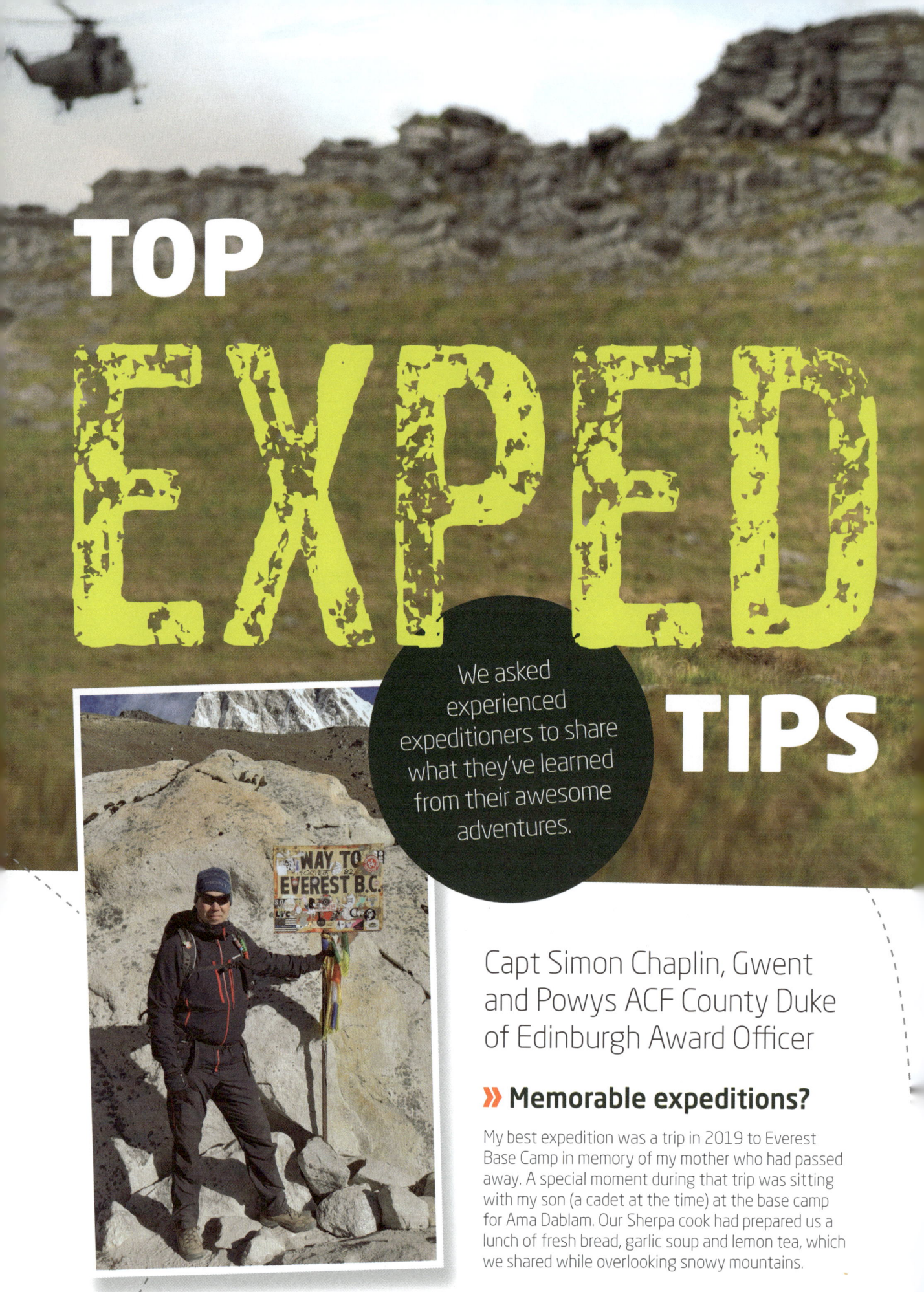

We asked experienced expeditioners to share what they've learned from their awesome adventures.

Capt Simon Chaplin, Gwent and Powys ACF County Duke of Edinburgh Award Officer

» Memorable expeditions?

My best expedition was a trip in 2019 to Everest Base Camp in memory of my mother who had passed away. A special moment during that trip was sitting with my son (a cadet at the time) at the base camp for Ama Dablam. Our Sherpa cook had prepared us a lunch of fresh bread, garlic soup and lemon tea, which we shared while overlooking snowy mountains.

CADET LIFE

Photo: Peter Russell

Another memorable moment was from an Army Cadets expedition, The Open Gold, which took place at Otterburn Camp last October. The group I was overseeing had to divert their route due to fallen trees in a forest so we missed each other for a checkpoint. I returned to my vehicle to find a note saying: 'Don't worry we R still alive', which made me chuckle and showed they could cope with anything.

'Don't worry, we R still alive ...'

»Favourite expedition/ camp game?

A good game I've played with cadets to fill time at camp and help the team gel is 'truth and lie'. One cadet picks someone they don't know in the team, then takes them somewhere the rest of the group can't hear their conversation and asks them for three statements about themselves: two that are true and one that's a lie. They then rejoin the team and introduce their new friend, giving the three bits of information, and the group has to decide which is the lie.

Gilly Moncur, SO3 Training Regional Command, and Diversity and Inclusion Adviser Scotland

» Most memorable expedition?

Climbing Kilimanjaro, which we did over eight days – five days' gradual climb to acclimatise, one day's final steep ascent and two days of rapid descent to avoid altitude sickness. The last kilometre along the ridge was literally one step in front of the other but being at the top (pictured – Gilly on the left) was amazing. Our heads were swimming with the altitude, exertion and euphoria.

» Tips for first-time expeditioners?

Try to get your map-reading skills as good as they can be before you go. Apps like Ordnance Survey are great but, if your phone battery runs out or there's no signal, you still need to know where you're going. Pack the right maps to cover the whole of your exped (I like 1:25,000 best for walking). Have a compass and know the basics of using it and study the map beforehand to get a feel for the route and terrain.

» What kit do you always pack?

A different pair of footwear for evenings in the camp (usually trainers or Crocs) to give my feet a breather. One of my personal luxuries is my map case, where I keep my maps and compass. It has a pocket for a pencil, emergency whistle and magnifying glass.

» Good expedition games?

A good one that helps everyone get to know each other is to ask each person to show the latest photo on their phone and reveal to the group why it's important to them.

» Your perfect exped snack?

A trail mix created from a packet of mixed fruit with cranberries and apricots to which I add some mixed nuts and seeds. I try to avoid snacks with artificial sugars if I can, and this one provides lots of energy.

Lt Gina Allsop,
Sports Officer and Adventure Training Officer at Sussex ACF

» Memorable expeditions?

The first was DofE when I was 13, which gave me my first taste of adventure and freedom. The second was with the Army: I was in the Army ski team and went on the tour leaders' course, where you go off-piste into backcountry. It was thrilling because we were going to places that people hadn't been for weeks and cutting our own tracks. At one point we got avalanched in and had to build a snow hole to sleep in before we could get ourselves out (pictured). That was character-building stuff!

» Essential kit?

If I'm doing a solo expedition, I always take my Garmin watch as it has all my maps and can also send a satellite signal if I fall or get stuck somewhere. I also take my phone, a spare pair of socks, a pack of cards and my favourite treat to boost energy levels and mood: a vegan "pork" pie.

» Advice for cadets on their first expedition?

Enjoy it! It'll be tough but it'll also be amazing. You'll get to meet new people and build connections. Pack your kit well in advance and do some short trial walks with it beforehand, so you can make sure it's comfortable.

» Other achievements?

At the end of April I did a Scotland 300, which started with a 100-mile walk of the West Highland Way with my full kit – on my own and unsupported. Then jumping in a kayak and paddling down a glen and then getting on a bike and cycling another 100 miles back. It was to raise money for ACCT UK.

'A vegan "pork" pie to boost my energy levels and mood'

'Getting a good night's sleep is key'

Liz Green, SO2 DofE

» Memorable trips?

I did my Gold DofE when I was 17. I was an Air Cadet and we did it in the Cairngorms over four days. It was a circular route and the sense of isolation was amazing. We saw lots of deer and birds of prey, had a great team and – most importantly – good food at the end of each day (especially puddings), which kept us going!

On one of the days, we met another group with an injured person. We helped them to get a helicopter to airlift them off the mountain. It was terrible for them but exciting for us to be involved.

» Tips for first-time expeditioners?

Aim to get into your sleeping bag dry and to keep any wet gear out of the way; you'll be so grateful for a warm bed. Also know how to cook a meal you're going to enjoy.

The most important thing of all, however, is to know what to do when something does go wrong – whether that's a blister or a broken shoelace or something more serious like an injury or getting lost. You need to understand what you can deal with yourself and when to ask for help.

» What kit do you always pack?

Getting a good night's sleep is key. I take a sleeping-bag liner and an inflatable pillow. If you can sleep in warmth and comfort you can deal with the challenges of the following day. Also take treats you like which'll perk you up.

CADET LIFE

Lt Col Richard Phillips, Deputy Commandant Kent ACF

» Memorable expeditions?

One was a solo trip following the Chemin de la Liberté (Freedom Trail), a five-day mountainous trek across the central Pyrenees from France into northern Spain. It was the route used by prisoners of war escaping to neutral Spain from German-occupied Europe during the Second World War. I saw very few people on the route, so maintaining my own safety was very important.

The second was an expedition during a half-term in 2018 when I took my two daughters (then aged 12 and 14) on a self-guided trek traversing Hadrian's Wall (pictured below) from Newcastle to Carlisle. It was fantastic to spend quality time with them and to complete an expedition I'd been trying to do but which kept being postponed due to operational commitments. The girls were apprehensive at the start, but they talk about it as one of the best things they've ever done.

'Cadets nearly always wish they'd packed lighter'

» Advice to cadets going on their first expedition?

Pack light! Take a look at everything in your rucksack and ask yourself if you really need it. That extra phone battery shouldn't be necessary if the phone is just for emergencies. An electric toothbrush is a bit of a luxury that won't be needed – just use a normal one. At the end of an expedition, I always ask cadets what they learnt and they nearly all wish they'd packed lighter.

» What would you never go without?

Lightweight flip-flops. After a long day trekking you need to give your feet some air.

Decoding CyberFirst

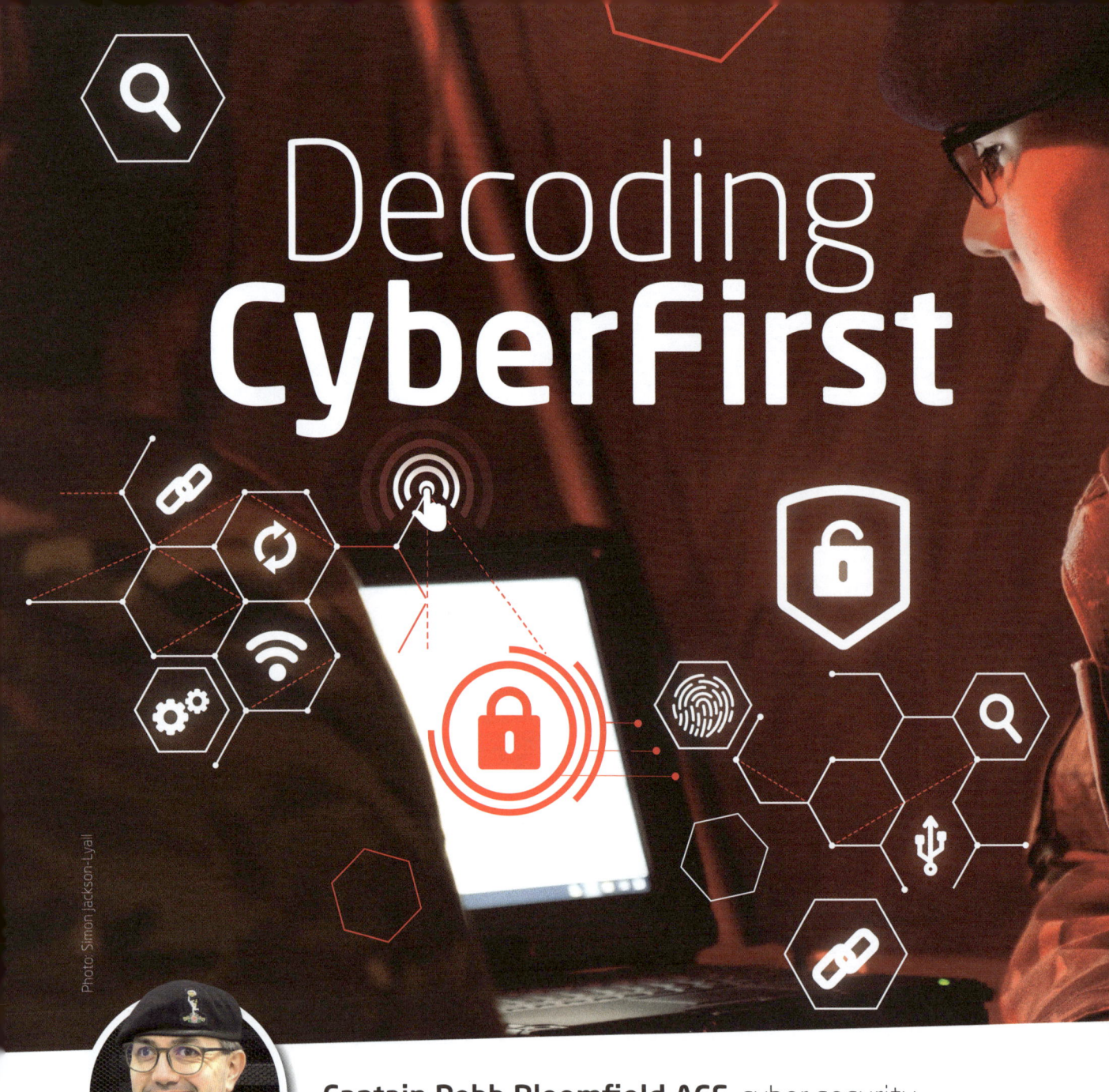

Captain Robb Bloomfield ACF, cyber security specialist and CyberFirst Project Officer in the Cadet CIS Training Team, decrypts the CyberFirst programme.

» What is the CyberFirst programme?

CyberFirst was set up by the National Cyber Security Centre to introduce young people to cyber security. The Army Cadets' CyberFirst programme differs from the public programme slightly as we only run three courses: Adventurers (a one-day course), Defenders and Advanced (both week-long residential courses). There are no age restrictions, but Defenders is a four-star-qualifying course so we'd expect cadets to be two-star complete to be eligible.

» How did you get involved with CyberFirst?

I joined the ACF in 2011 and became involved with the CIS Training Team when I went on a radio training course. It just so happened that the team was developing a cyber course at the time and I was able to join the discussions, which turned into planning for the launch of CyberFirst. Within a month, we were running the first CyberFirst course. I've been the CyberFirst Project Officer in the Cadet CIS Training Team at Blandford Camp for four years now.

CADET LIFE

'You become far more motivated to take control of your own cyber security'

Cadets taking part in EX Rolling Thunder 2019

Capt Robb Bloomfield ACF at a CyberFirst Defenders course at Blandford in 2018

» Were you into IT as a teenager?

I spent a lot of time hanging out with my mates, listening to heavy metal and playing my guitar! I didn't want to go to university and had no specific career aspirations until an IT teacher at school asked me to help fix some computers in my lunch breaks. I realised I liked the technical challenge of understanding how they worked and I particularly enjoyed helping people by creating effective systems and secure networks for them to use.

» How did you progress to a career in cyber security?

As soon as I left school I was employed as the school's IT technician. Following a degree course with The Open University, I moved into cyber security and am now the principal cyber-security engineer for a major global logistics company. I help ensure many of the components and products used in our everyday lives get to where they need to be, without disruption or delay. When you consider how many items are moving around the planet all day, every day, and all the related automated processes, it makes for an interesting job.

» What can cadets expect from Adventurers?

The Adventurers course introduces cadets to the breadth of cyber by raising their awareness of how data is used. It's far more than an e-safety course. They'll use open-source intelligence gathering to solve a problem and work in teams to crack codes. And they'll explore data more creatively in topics such as website creation and data analysis in sport.

Words like 'coding' and 'data' can sound geeky but data is a huge and interconnected part of our lives, which is why cyber security is so important. Adventurers demystifies this and empowers cadets to get involved.

» What happens on the Defenders course?

The Defenders course tightens the focus on cyber security and offers cadets the chance to get more hands-on with the tech, so they can learn how to protect themselves online.

They work in a team to build a network that mimics a home network, with a broadband router and a web cam, which is connected to another team to simulate the internet. The exercise enables them to safely witness what happens when your network is vulnerable and your camera can be accessed by someone outside your home network.

It's all very well being told you need to be careful online, but when you see how something works and how it can be compromised, you become far more motivated to take control of your own cyber security. Defenders gives cadets the skills to do this.

» Who would benefit from the Advanced course?

The Advanced course takes things a step further and introduces digital forensics, which includes carrying out investigations and trying to recover lost or apparently deleted data. It also covers exploring encryption technologies and looking at the broader career opportunities in and around cyber security.

Cadets who complete the Advanced course will have in-depth knowledge of cyber security, making them an asset to any workplace, whatever the role. If they're considering a career in cyber security, completing the Advanced course will also help them stand out when applying for work experience, apprenticeships, university places or bursaries.

» Can anyone join a CyberFirst course?

All cadets are welcome. The CyberFirst programme is free, and the tech is accessible during the courses so it doesn't matter if cadets don't have a computer at home. We make sure all cadets feel welcome and engaged, regardless of their skills, hobbies, background or confidence level.

Diversity within a cyber security team is key to its success. We all have different life experiences, interests, abilities and perspectives. These help teams to analyse threats – including how, why, when and where they may arise – and better understand the mindset and behaviour of the people we're trying to protect.

» What are the career opportunities in cyber security?

Cyber security offers lots of opportunities as it's a rapidly growing field that affects almost every aspect of our lives. Even if you don't enjoy STEM subjects at school, don't rule it out.

Global cyber security requires complex legislation and regulation, creating opportunities for lawyers. Farming is increasingly using GPS technology and automation, so there's a demand in cyber security for people with knowledge of agriculture. Expertise in psychology, sociology, politics or economics is also helpful in understanding threats and the motivation behind them.

» Why would you recommend CyberFirst to cadets?

When we don't understand something it can seem intimidating, and this certainly applies to cyber security.

The knowledge cadets develop through the CyberFirst programme gives them confidence online and elsewhere in their lives. They feel empowered to share their knowledge of cyber security with friends and family, because they've learned that our cyber defence is only as strong as the weakest link. Any one of us could be that link, but attending a CyberFirst course means it's less likely to be you and sharing our knowledge makes us stronger collectively.

Cadets taking part in Ex Rolling Thunder 2019

Photo: Simon Jackson-Lyall

Photo: Kate Knight

CADET LIFE

You might begin by strengthening a friend's social media privacy settings or helping your nan spot a phishing scam, but you could end up knowledge-sharing as part of a cutting-edge, code-cracking team at Government Communication Headquarters (GCHQ). It all starts with CyberFirst!

'They'll use open-source intelligence gathering to solve a problem and work in teams to crack codes'

Go further

Scan the QR code to find out more about CyberFirst.

Cadets interested in taking part in the CyberFirst programme should firstly take a look at the courses available on the cadet portal and then speak to their detachment commander.

CyberFirst

Photo: Simon Jackson-Lyall

First aid HEROES

A whopping 37,000 cadets and CFAVs have completed first-aid qualifications in the past 12 months, and some of them have heroically put their skills to use in real-life emergencies.

Every cadet receives training in life-saving first aid skills so they can make a difference in the event of an accident or emergency. There are many stories of brave actions carried out by cadets and CFAVs, which have in some cases saved lives. We showcase some of the first aiders who've been nominated this year for ACCT UK's Praiseworthy Action Certificate after responding to a medical emergency.

Meet the heroes

Cdt LCpl Soumya Joshi, Buckinghamshire ACF, resuscitated her grandmother when she collapsed at home. She provided cardiopulmonary resuscitation (CPR) until paramedics arrived and took over. Soumya's grandmother was taken to hospital but sadly never regained consciousness and passed away two days later. However, in those two days the rest of the family were able to come and say goodbye, which would not have been possible without Soumya's heroic actions.

Cdt Zara Laws, 1st Battalion The Highlanders ACF, showed her first aid competence in two incidents. Firstly, she and a fellow cadet performed first aid on a member of the public who was unconscious. They called an ambulance and stayed on the scene until it arrived. In the second incident, Zara found her mum on the kitchen floor in a lot of pain and struggling to breathe. She called an ambulance and stayed with her mum, talking to her and keeping her calm on the way to hospital.

Cdt Peter Cordwell, Bedfordshire and Hertfordshire ACF, has been his father's sole carer (his dad uses a wheelchair and has epilepsy) since Peter was nine years old. Earlier this year, his father had a particularly bad seizure, so Peter placed him in the recovery position and protected his head from injury before administering his medication. He then called an ambulance and gave paramedics the details of his dad's care plan.

Cdt Cpl Daniel Quinn, Dorchester Detachment, Dorset ACF, saved his mum's life when she stopped breathing after choking on some food. As she began to lose consciousness, Daniel administered back slaps and abdominal thrusts. Fortunately, the third cycle of these shifted the obstruction and she managed to gasp some breath and cough out the food. After the incident, Daniel insisted his mum go to hospital to get checked by medical specialists.

CFAV SSI Austin Snelson, Warrington Detachment, Cheshire ACF, went to the aid of a rugby player who had suffered a cardiac arrest on the pitch. He and an off-duty nurse took charge, started chest compressions and sent for a defibrillator. They managed to restore the casualty's breathing before the ambulance arrived.

Cdt Cpl Poppy Jess, Lisnagarvey High School CCF, aided a woman at a bus stop who had collapsed. Poppy called an ambulance and stayed with the casualty as she regained consciousness. She provided reassurance to the woman and took her medical history before handing over to the paramedics.

Cdt LCpl Jay Pybus and **Cdt LCpl Duncan Brown, 1st Battalion The Highlanders ACF**, used their first aid skills to treat a fellow cadet who was suffering from heatstroke during a company training weekend. They helped him rehydrate and took him to his accommodation where they placed wet towels on his forehead. They checked on the casualty regularly during breaks in their training.

First aid in numbers

32,769

Number of first-aid qualifications undertaken by cadets in 12 months.

4,842

Number of CFAVs to complete first aid training courses in 12 months.

CFAV SSI Naomi Lee, Buckinghamshire ACF, ran to the aid of a rider who had fallen off their horse and was screaming in pain. They had suffered a punctured lung, fractured ribs and a brain bleed. When paramedics arrived, Naomi handed over to them and assisted in moving the casualty across a field to the waiting ambulance.

Cdt Ennis Cotterhill-Stirling, 1st Battalion The Highlanders ACF, leapt into action when a fellow cadet suffered an accident while mountain biking. Ennis cleaned his injured face, applied a dressing and reassured the casualty before he was taken to A&E for stitches.

CFAV Lt Christopher Cooper, Cardiff and Vale College CCF, went to the aid of a man who collapsed from cardiac arrest when out shopping. Christopher administered CPR to the man and managed to restore his breathing.

Cdt Heather Mowat, 1st Battalion The Highlanders ACF, ran to the aid of a young boy who was struck in the head by a car door caught by the wind. The youngster was crying and in distress, so Heather checked him for injuries and offered reassurance to the child and his parents.

Cpl Nadine Miller, Glasgow and Lanarkshire ACF, was on a coy camp when she noticed another cadet was unwell. When the cadet lost consciousness, Nadine quickly put her in the recovery position. When the ambulance arrived, she calmly handed over to paramedics and stayed with the casualty while they were treated.

CFAV SI Séamus Ferry, Glasgow and Lanarkshire ACF, heard screaming and looked out of his window to see that a neighbour had tripped and fallen down a storm bunker. Séamus ran down five flights of stairs to assist. He called the emergency services and stayed with the casualty until they arrived and then assisted with the recovery operation.

Cdt Amelia Adams and **Cdt LCpl Perry Cavinue, Glasgow and Lanarkshire ACF**, were shopping when a woman collapsed and had a seizure. The cadets stepped up and took control, working together to ensure the casualty was safe and her head was protected. They remained calm and provided reassurance to shop staff and members of the public that they were both first aiders, before handing over to paramedics.

CFAV Pl Nadine Howard, Bedfordshire and Hertfordshire ACF, witnessed a car drive into a stationary vehicle and immediately went to help. She found an initially unresponsive woman who was lapsing in and out of consciousness and complaining of severe pain to her back and neck. The CFAV climbed into the car to support her and remained there until paramedics arrived 45 minutes later.

CFAV Pl Sam Gravell, Bedfordshire and Hertfordshire ACF, administered first aid to a man who was in a great deal of pain and having an asthma attack after an accident at work. Sam sent for his inhaler and called an ambulance. He then supported the casualty's head and neck until paramedics arrived.

> **'Breathing was restored and the baby recovered, thanks to Lucy's quick thinking'**

Cdt Max Thurbon, Bedfordshire and Hertfordshire ACF, went to the aid of a fellow pupil at his school who had slipped on mud and badly cut his calf. He arranged an ambulance, dressed the wound and immobilised the leg.

CFAV SI Lucy Baines, Lancashire ACF, encountered a panicking woman with a lifeless baby. She immediately dialled 999 and started CPR. The paramedics arrived after 15-20 minutes and asked Lucy to continue CPR. Breathing was restored and the baby recovered thanks to Lucy's quick thinking and brave actions.

Cdt Olive McGreal, Bedfordshire and Hertfordshire ACF, was in her CTC barracks when she came across a fellow cadet in distress and choking on some crisps. She quickly administered back blows until the casualty began breathing normally again.

CADET LIFE

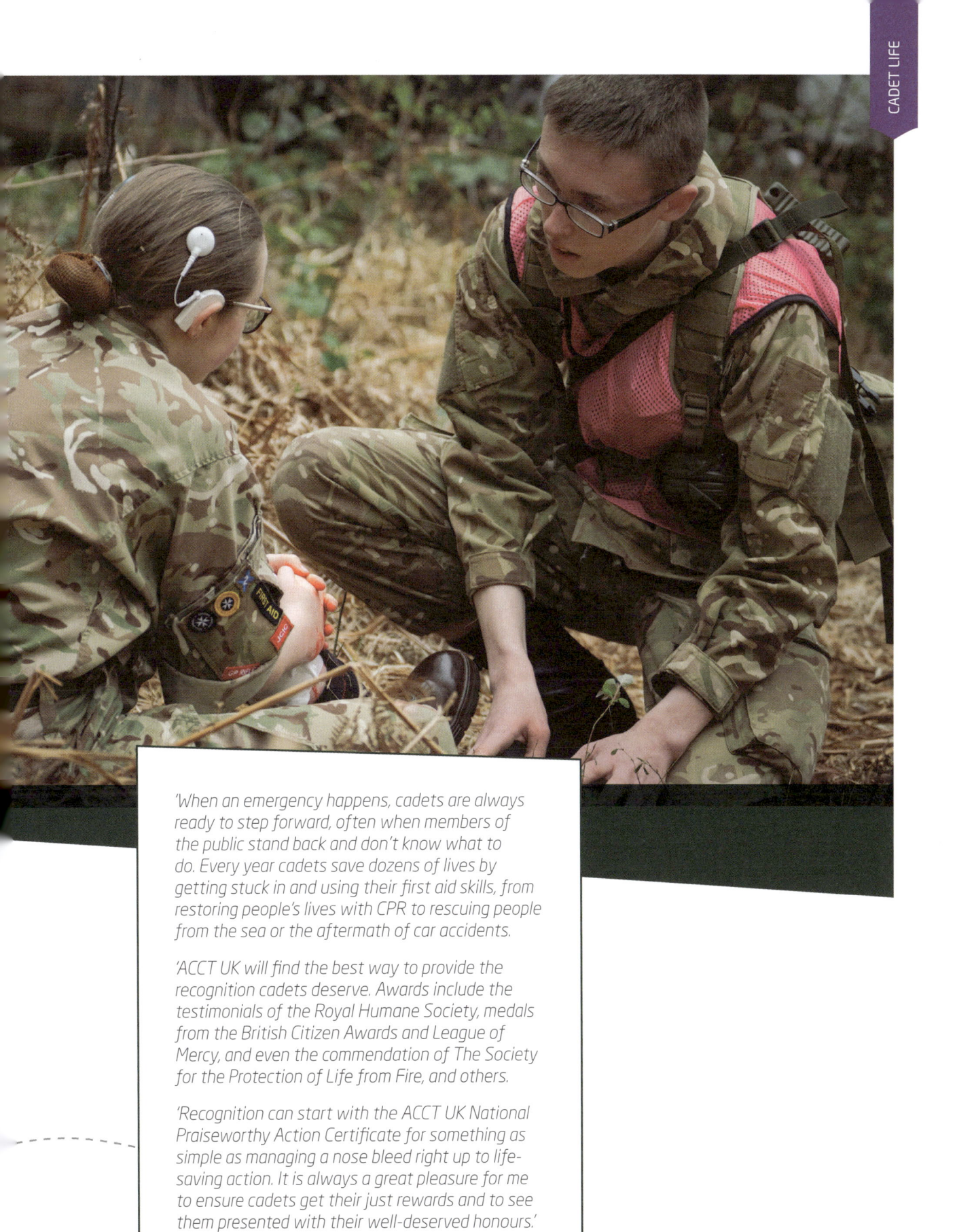

'When an emergency happens, cadets are always ready to step forward, often when members of the public stand back and don't know what to do. Every year cadets save dozens of lives by getting stuck in and using their first aid skills, from restoring people's lives with CPR to rescuing people from the sea or the aftermath of car accidents.

'ACCT UK will find the best way to provide the recognition cadets deserve. Awards include the testimonials of the Royal Humane Society, medals from the British Citizen Awards and League of Mercy, and even the commendation of The Society for the Protection of Life from Fire, and others.

'Recognition can start with the ACCT UK National Praiseworthy Action Certificate for something as simple as managing a nose bleed right up to life-saving action. It is always a great pleasure for me to ensure cadets get their just rewards and to see them presented with their well-deserved honours.'

Alan Sharkey, Honours and Awards Manager, Army Cadet Charitable Trust UK (ACCT)

Cdt Gerard Evans, Bedfordshire and Hertfordshire ACF, witnessed a man get struck by a car and hit his head on a kerb. The casualty was knocked unconscious and had shallow breathing and blood coming from his nose and head. With the help of a bystander, Gerard administered first aid and reassured the casualty as he regained consciousness until paramedics arrived.

> *'The casualty was knocked unconscious and had shallow breathing and blood coming from his nose and head'*

Cdt Cpl Ilaria Grimason, Northern Ireland Battalion ACF, was on her way to an exam when she came across a girl lying on the ground unresponsive. A friend said she had fainted, hitting her head on the way down, causing a head wound and a brief loss of consciousness. Ilaria applied pressure to the wound with tissues and put the casualty in the recovery position until relieved by the school nurse.

Cdt Staff Sgt Joshua Adams-Piggott, Bedfordshire and Hertfordshire ACF, rushed to the aid of his father when he tripped and fell down the stairs in the early hours of the morning. Joshua applied pressure to a wound on his father's head and then drove him to the hospital when the ambulance was delayed.

Cdt LCpl Imogen Hully, Gwent & Powys AFC, used her first aid skills when her sister suffered a seizure in Cyprus. Having just completed her 2 star First Aid Course the week before, Imogen sought medical aid and directed her siblings on how they could help.

Cdt Connor Jones, Bedfordshire and Hertfordshire ACF, was playing basketball when his friend collapsed from exhaustion. He put him in the recovery position and waited until he recovered. He then took him to the local railway station and travelled with him to his home before leaving him in his mother's care.

CFAV Pl Samuel Burkitt, South West London ACF, jumped into action when a woman had a seizure at a railway station and caught her head between two posts. Samuel managed to free the casualty and administer first aid.

CFAV SI Sam Hilder and **CFAV SI Cavan Wootton, Lincolnshire ACF**, were walking back from a parade event when they came across a woman who had attempted to take her own life. They took control of the situation, assessed her injuries, covered her in a foil blanket and administered first aid until the paramedics arrived.

CFAV SI Ali Gotto, Middlesex and North West London ACF, was at a family gathering when someone started to choke on their food. He administered two cycles of back blows and abdominal thrusts before the food was partially dislodged and the casualty taken to hospital.

CFAV Lt Anthony Jemmot, Middlesex and North West London ACF, was travelling on the Eurostar near Lille when a call went out for medical assistance. A passenger was in severe pain and almost unresponsive. He administered first aid and looked after the woman until an ambulance arrived.

Cdt Savana Pritchard, Norfolk ACF, rushed to her sister's aid when she cut her finger badly while cooking dinner. Savana got her on to her back on the floor, raised her feet and applied pressure to the wound before calling 999.

Cdt LCpl Kenneth Barrett, Cdt LCpl Arwin Bool, Cdt LCpl Aleksandra Angom and **Cdt LCpl Jessica King,** all **Middlesex and North West London ACF**, were in McDonald's after a cadet event when they saw staff with a customer who had vomited and was struggling to breath. The cadets took charge of the incident, clearing the vomit from the man's airway before placing him in the recovery position. They then waited with the casualty until emergency services arrived.

CADET LIFE

what3words

what3words is an invaluable app to have on your phone in a first aid emergency. It divides the world into 3 metre squares and each square has a unique combination of three words. When it's hard to pinpoint where you are, simply read out the three words assigned to your location and the emergency services can find you. Download free on the App Store or Google Play.

Go further

Each year, cadets and CFAVs from across the UK take part in the National First Aid Competition, which involves life-like emergency scenarios. This year the national competition will take place at Holcombe Moor on 3-5 November. Each regional area has a place for an ACF cadet team, an ACF young adult team, a CCF cadet team and a CCF young adult team. Contact your CFATO (ACF) or Bde Rep (CCF) to find out more.

HYDRATION 101

Keeping hydrated is one of the most important ways to maintain a healthy body. **Terry Hayter, SO2 Sports and Physical Development** at HQ Regional Command, expands on the advice in the *Keeping Active Training Manual*.

» Why we need water

It may be surprising to learn that water makes up 60 per cent of the human body. Water is needed for a wide range of processes within the body, for example it's used by the kidneys to flush out waste and toxins via urine, helps the digestive system function properly, keeps joints lubricated, and is used by the circulatory system to help carry essential nutrients, oxygen and glucose to cells.

» Hydration and exercise

Water is also important for regulating the body's temperature and preventing dehydration. When it's hot, water is lost through sweat which helps to keep the body cool. This is why you should drink more when you're hot after exercising, or in a hot climate, as lost fluids need to be replaced.

» How to stay hydrated

The best way to stay hydrated is to drink around two litres of fluids each day (roughly eight glasses). While water is the best source of hydration because it has no calories or sugars, your daily fluid intake can also be obtained from other drinks such as milk and sugar-free drinks.

It's worth noting that you don't need to consume sports or electrolyte drinks to improve physical performance. Eating a balanced diet should provide and replace all the electrolytes and nutrition you need. You won't need to get more through drinks or supplements, which often contain added sugars.

» Striking a balance

While good hydration is essential, it's worth bearing in mind that it is possible to overhydrate if you drink too much. Overhydration causes an imbalance in the body's electrolytes. Signs of overhydration include nausea and vomiting, headaches, fatigue, confusion or disorientation, and muscle cramps.

» Check your urine

One of the simplest ways to make sure you're staying hydrated is to check the colour of your urine. Very pale yellow urine is a good sign and means you're staying hydrated, but darker yellow/brown urine suggests you are dehydrated and need to drink more.

'The human body is made up of up to 60 per cent water'

Go further

The topic of hydration will feature in a new upcoming Army Cadets *Healthy Eating* video.

The film will be a useful resource if you want to find out more about the foods you should eat and the ones to avoid to maintain a balanced diet.

Army Cadets is also releasing a *Keeping Active* video, which will cover moderate physical training including exercises you can do at home in your own time.

Keep your eyes peeled in future issues of *Army Cadet Magazine* for details of where to find the videos.

DIY flavour-filled fluids

Water is so good for you, but if you find it too bland here are some ways to make it more exciting.

Get fruity

Adding fresh slices of strawberry, lemon, lime, orange or cucumber to your water bottle will enhance the flavour, as will fresh mint or ginger.

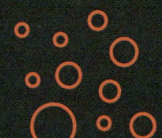

Spritz it up

If you're bored of still water, try sparkling instead. Opt for sparkling mineral water which has been carbonated at source and has nothing added to it. Or add some fizz yourself at home using a sparkling-water maker, such as a SodaStream.

Ice, ice baby

If room-temperature tap water doesn't appeal, adding ice can make it more thirst quenching. Get creative by freezing chunks of kiwi or melon or adding frozen berries to your drink for an additional fruity, icy hit.

SPOTLIGHT ON ...

THE ULYSSES TRUST

Army Cadets is supported by a number of incredible charities. We shine a light on the fantastic work of The Ulysses Trust, which enables cadets to gain life skills through access to adventurous training activities.

» Mission

The Ulysses Trust's mission is to provide financial assistance, encouragement and guidance to support challenging expeditions and adventurous activities planned and undertaken by the volunteer reserve and cadet forces of the UK.

Since its inception, the charity has raised more than £3.6 million to support over 41,000 individuals in over 3,030 expeditions. His Majesty King Charles III is the charity's patron.

» Benefits

The charity aims to enhance force and unit morale, recruitment, retention and public esteem. It also helps develop an individual's leadership, teamwork, confidence, courage, initiative, self-discipline and judgement.

The Trust supports adventurous training expeditions because of its potential to give young people valuable life skills, including teamwork and physical wellbeing.

'Adventure, particularly at a young age, is almost always a transformational experience,' said explorer, author and The Ulysses Trust Ambassador Levison Wood. 'Last year marked the 30th anniversary of The Ulysses Trust: 30 years of giving young people the opportunity to test themselves and learn what they are capable of.'

CADET LIFE

'Adventure is almost always a transformational experience'

» Vision

To bring the benefits of challenging, adventurous and community-related expeditions within the financial reach of every member of the UK's volunteer reserve and cadet forces.

» Eligibility

All cadet forces are eligible to apply for a grant to help fund an expedition. Expeditions must be sponsored by a Unit or HQ and have ACEATFA or other appropriate authorisation.

Post-pandemic, The Ulysses Trust relaxed its requirements for grants and provided more funds to assist activities specifically for disadvantaged young people. This move saw a dramatic increase in the number of expeditions and participants supported.

» A Trust grant results in brilliant gains

A CCF unit was on the verge of collapse before involvement from The Ulysses Trust saw a turnaround in its popularity.

The Pioneer Secondary Academy CCF unit in Stoke Poges, Buckinghamshire, was set up in 2017 through the Cadet Expansion Programme (CEP) but gained little momentum at first.

An expedition to Snowdonia National Park was proposed as a game-changing initiative to revive the slow-growing unit. The prospect of adventure was a strong incentive for cadets and CFAVs to get involved, but it was a £5,796 grant from The Ulysses Trust that guaranteed it went ahead and was affordable for all.

The build-up included 12 exercises – mostly AT – which ensured the unit was well prepared. In July 2022, 24 cadets deployed to Snowdonia with four CFAVs. They engaged in challenging activities which pushed them out of their comfort zones, including a two-day wild camping expedition and a canoe journey down the estuary which ended with an evening campfire on the beach.

'I did things I thought I would never do, such as jumping in the water,' said **Cdt LCpl Nicola Chumber**. *'I can't swim but challenged myself and took the chance to complete every single opportunity that was given to me.'*

Following the expedition, the unit doubled in size – a direct result of the expedition and the charity's help.

'An expedition to Snowdonia National Park was a game-changing initiative'

Cadets from The Pioneer Secondary Academy CCF at Snowdonia National Park

» The sky's the limit

Skydiving remains a bucket-list fantasy for many but, thanks to a two-year fundraising campaign and donations from The Ulysses Trust, nine Norfolk ACF cadets became qualified skydivers in 2022.

Initially planned as a two-week residential skydiving expedition in Spain in 2020, plans were scuppered by the pandemic. The expedition eventually took place at Skydive Hibaldstow in north Lincolnshire in April 2022.

Cadets and CFAVs were overcome by the once-in-a-lifetime experience: *'I personally don't believe the exped could have been any better,'* said **Cdt LCpl Micah Bailey**. Expedition leader **Maj John Stopford-Pickering** appreciated the part The Ulysses Trust played in the process: *'We are all very grateful to The Ulysses Trust and our other donors for their support which helped to make this expedition possible.'*

» The Ulysses Trust Expedition Awards

Each year, The Ulysses Trust presents three awards for the finest expeditions (showcasing the best in leadership, challenge, courage and planning) among cadet forces, university units and volunteer reserve forces.

Last year's cadet category winner was Round the Island (pictured above). This yacht race round the Isle of Wight from 24–26 June was completed by UTC Reading CCF and funded by The Ulysses Trust.

'This is making-memories kind of stuff; we'll not forget this for the rest of our lives,' said Year 11 student **Mutahira Sheikh**.

Go further

Discover upcoming adventures taking place with the help of The Ulysses Trust, and apply for grants, by scanning the QR code.

Scan the QR codes to check out two epic videos from the dive.

www.ulyssestrust.co.uk

SPOTLIGHT ON ...

Army Cadet Charitable Trust UK

Discover more about the charity that enables access to life-changing opportunities within the ACF, ensuring all young people have the chance to develop and achieve.

» What does ACCT UK do?

ACCT UK is a national youth charity that opens up opportunities for young people in the Army Cadet Force by offering grants to support various activities. The charity supports over 34,000 cadets every year.

» What sort of activities?

Absolutely anything that helps young people develop physical, mental and social skills that will help them achieve their goals and give them the best possible start in life. That could be through music, sports, education or skills for life.

The charity provides funding that supports an individual life-changing activity (like an Army Cadet representing Team GB at the Olympics) right through to providing essential equipment needed for a new activity being developed by an Army Cadet group.

» What about CFAVs?

ACCT UK appreciates the immense value of Army Cadet volunteers, and supports them by working in partnership with CVQO to award bursaries to support CFAVs enrolled on leadership courses. This enables them to develop their professional skills in order to progress in their Army Cadets career and provide the best experience for their cadets.

» CFAV support

In partnership with Care First, ACCT UK has helped provide a substantial support system for CFAVs, including:

- 24/7 professional counselling, offering confidential support for issues that arise at home or at work. This is available to ACF adult volunteers and their families. Phone 0800 174319 if you need to talk to someone. Alternatively, there is an online platform CFAVs can access using their card with login details (if not received, contact enquiries@acctuk.org)

- An app to self-monitor health and encourage healthy behaviours

- Online financial tools

- Weekly webinars and articles

'Grants help cadets take part in activities which develop life skills and confidence'

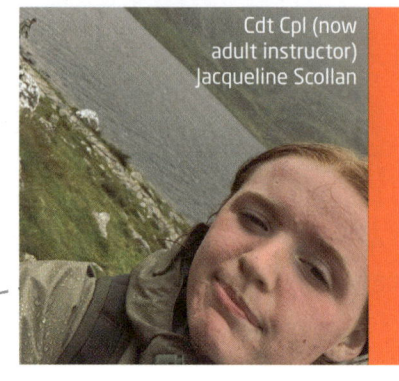

Cdt Cpl (now adult instructor) Jacqueline Scollan

» What grants are available through ACCT UK?

County grants

ACCT UK supports Army Cadets Counties in helping fund equipment beyond that usually funded by the chain of command.

Individual grants

These grants help individual cadets take part in activities that develop life skills and confidence, such as adventurous training, DofE expeditions, battlefield tours and overseas events. It could reduce the cost for a whole group or make an activity affordable for an individual cadet.

Professional development grants

ACCT UK believes in developing the skills of Army Cadets volunteers to enable them to thrive in their role. Working in partnership with CVQO, these bursaries support CFAVs enrolled on the ILM Level 4 Leadership and Management through to the Initial Officer Training Course.

Other grants

ACCT UK also helps fund activities that enhance cadet training programmes and activities related to adventure training, sports, music, first aid, DofE and battlefield tours.

The Matthew Bacon Bursary

The Matthew Bacon Bursary enables individual army cadets to take part in a life-changing 19-day Outward Bound Trust (OBT) expedition which would otherwise be beyond their financial means. It is open to cadets who lack confidence, are from a disadvantaged background or have experienced difficulties, with the aim of boosting emotional health and wellbeing by discovering new skills and enjoying a thrilling adventure.

The bursary has transformed the lives of more than 60 cadets to date. It was set up in memory of Major Matthew Bacon, an officer in the Intelligence Corps, who was killed while on tour in Iraq on 11 September 2005. In Matthew's honour, his family set up the fund to help young cadets who could benefit from additional support in order to develop and achieve.

'Two weeks with Outward Bound has been the best thing I've ever done,' said Cdt Cpl (now adult instructor) Jacqueline Scollan, Glasgow & Lanarkshire ACF, one of the 2022 participants. 'I met so many people from all over the world. While on the course I learnt lots of new skills and even decided to go into the outdoor industry – I'm now studying Adventure Sports at college. This simply would never have been possible without the Matthew Bacon Bursary.'

» ACCT UK Awards

ACCT UK recognises the contributions of cadets and adult volunteers both within the ACF and the community. To celebrate these achievements, it holds internal and external national award nominations and events.

Each year the charity organises an Excellence Awards ceremony, which hosts VIPs and award winners who have excelled in the areas of DofE, sport, music, first aid and community service.

The ACCT UK Excellence Awards 2023 (pictured below and supported by BAE Systems) were held in London in June, with the winners as follows:

Duke of Edinburgh's Award
Cdt Sgt Ezri Spring (Kent ACF)
Maj (retd) Alan Thompson (Northumbria ACF)

First Aid
Cdt CSgt Dawson Whitelegg (Bedfordshire and Hertfordshire ACF)
Staff Sgt Instructor Amanda Wixon (Greater London South East Sector ACF)

Music
Cdt CSM Nicole Pennington (Greater Manchester ACF)
2nd Lt Callum Mellis (51 Brigade, Black Watch Bn Scotland ACF)

Sport
Cdt Cpl Dylan Perkin (Clwyd and Gwynedd ACF)
Capt Rachael Jones (Gwent and Powys ACF)

Community Service (donor: Ammo & Co)
Cdt Cpl William Callaghan (Yorkshire North and West ACF)
2nd Lt Michael Stokes and 2nd Lt Sarah Stokes (Gloucestershire ACF)

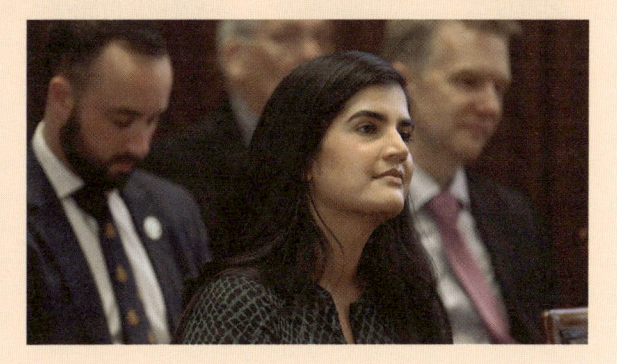

Cadet Forces MEDALS

The Cadet Forces Medal is awarded to commissioned officers and non-commissioned adult instructors of the UK Cadet Forces in recognition of long and efficient service. Clasps are issued for every six additional years. Huge congratulations to everyone included in this October 2022 to September 2023 roundup.

6TH CLASP

Maj	M	WOOTTON	ACF	Yorkshire (North & West) ACF

5TH CLASP

Lt Col	M	PASSMORE	ACF	Angus & Dundee Battalion ACF
Maj	J	BURNS	ACF	Cumbria ACF
Maj	M	SCOTT	ACF	Durham ACF
SMI	A	SCOTT	ACF	Humberside & South Yorkshire ACF
Capt	P	BRISTER	CCF	Kings School (Grantham) CCF
Maj	N	ATHERTON	ACF	Nottinghamshire ACF
SMI	P	COLLINS	ACF	Wiltshire ACF

4TH CLASP

Maj	J	READ	ACF	1st (Northern Ireland) Battalion ACF
Lt Col	R	LOCKHART	ACF	Argyll & Sutherland Highlanders Battalion ACF
Col	D	COULTER	ACF	Glasgow & Lanarkshire Battalion ACF
SMI	M	WELLINGTON	ACF	Gloucestershire ACF (The Rifles)
Capt	A	SMITH	ACF	Hampshire & Isle of Wight ACF
Col	M	DAVANNA	ACF	Leicestershire, Northamptonshire & Rutland ACF
SMI	G	BYRNE	ACF	Merseyside ACF
Maj	D	WOOLCOTT	CCF	Royal Grammar School (Guildford) CCF

Rank	Initial	Surname	Org	Unit
Capt	K	FRITH	ACF	Staffordshire & West Midlands North Sector ACF
Col	H	STAMBOULIEH	ACF	The City & County of Bristol ACF
Lt Col	A	NOTICE	ACF	Warwickshire & West Midlands South Sector ACF
SMI	P	SHAW	ACF	Yorkshire (North & West) ACF

3RD CLASP

Rank	Initial	Surname	Org	Unit
SMI	D	RILEY	ACF	Staffordshire & West Midlands North Sector ACF
RSMI	J	JOHNSTON	ACF	1st (Northern Ireland) Battalion ACF
SMI	B	FARQUHAR	ACF	1st (Northern Ireland) Battalion ACF
Maj	S	BLAIR	ACF	Argyll & Sutherland Highlanders Battalion ACF
SSI	C	ENGLISH	ACF	Bedfordshire & Hertfordshire ACF
SMI	C	BURN	ACF	Cleveland ACF
SSI	M	CRAVEN	ACF	Clwyd & Gwynedd ACF
Maj	T	COOPER	ACF	Clwyd & Gwynedd ACF
Col	M	THOMSETT	ACF	Dorset ACF
Col	N	FOSTER	ACF	Durham ACF
Maj	E	SOKOLOWSKI	ACF	Greater London South West Sector ACF
SSI	A	COWLARD	ACF	Greater London South West Sector ACF
Maj	N	FOSTER	ACF	Hampshire & Isle of Wight ACF
Lt	J	SEAMAN	CCF	King Edward VI Grammar School (Chelmsford) CCF
Maj	K	HEALD	ACF	Lancashire ACF
SMI	S	GILBEY	ACF	Leicestershire, Northamptonshire & Rutland ACF
Capt	M	ELLISON	ACF	Nottinghamshire ACF
Lt	P	CHURCHER	ACF	Nottinghamshire ACF
SMI	D	BATCHELOR	ACF	Royal County of Berkshire ACF
Maj	S	WARREN	ACF	Royal County of Berkshire ACF
SMI	J	MURPHY	ACF	Somerset Cadet Battalion (The Rifles) ACF
Maj	C	PICKIN	ACF	Staffordshire & West Midlands North Sector ACF
Maj	S	DAVISON	ACF	Suffolk ACF
SSI	D	GILLETT	ACF	Warwickshire & West Midlands South Sector ACF
Maj	R	MURRAY	ACF	Yorkshire (North & West) ACF

2ND CLASP

Rank	Initial	Surname	Org	Unit
RSMI	T	KIRKHAM	ACF	1st (Northern Ireland) Battalion ACF
Maj	D	GILLESPIE	ACF	1st (Northern Ireland) Battalion ACF
Capt	B	STEVENSON	ACF	Argyll & Sutherland Highlanders Battalion ACF
Capt	J	DALEY	ACF	Buckinghamshire (The Rifles) ACF
Col	S	RAMSEY	ACF	Cleveland ACF
SMI	S	HINE	ACF	Cumbria ACF
SMI	P	SIMPSON	ACF	Durham ACF
Lt	M	COLLINS	ACF	Glasgow & Lanarkshire Battalion ACF
SMI	D	THOMAS	ACF	Gloucestershire ACF (The Rifles)
Lt	C	CANDLER	ACF	Gloucestershire ACF (The Rifles)
Capt	M	SLADE	ACF	Gloucestershire ACF (The Rifles)
Lt	T	BENNETT	ACF	Gloucestershire ACF (The Rifles)
Capt	M	THORNE	ACF	Greater Manchester ACF
SSI	P	CLEMENTS	ACF	Gwent & Powys ACF
SMI	D	WESTALL	ACF	Kent ACF
SMI	P	CASS	ACF	Kent ACF
SMI	K	MASON	ACF	Lancashire ACF
Lt Col	J	ECCLES	ACF	Lancashire ACF
Maj	J	SCRASE	ACF	Lancashire ACF
Lt Col	B	KAVANAGH	ACF	Merseyside ACF
SSI	N	ANNABLE	ACF	Nottinghamshire ACF
SMI	D	BROWN	ACF	Oxfordshire (The Rifles) Battalion ACF
Capt	J	LEE	ACF	Oxfordshire (The Rifles) Battalion ACF
Maj	W	THRUSSELL	ACF	Oxfordshire (The Rifles) Battalion ACF
Col	M	SHALLOW	ACF	Royal County of Berkshire ACF
RSMI	S	PELLING	ACF	Sussex ACF
SSI	A	GREENWOOD	ACF	The West Lowland Battalion ACF
Maj	T	STOKES	ACF	Wiltshire ACF
RSMI	R	HEARN	ACF	Wiltshire ACF

1ST CLASP

Rank	Initial	Surname	Org	Unit
Pl	B	DHILLON	ACF	Buckinghamshire (The Rifles) ACF
Lt	A	VINTNER		11 Inf Bde & HQ SE Non Effective Officers Pool
SSI	C	HOLCOMBE		11 Inf Bde & HQ SE Non Effective Other Ranks Pool
SSI	G	MCKELVEY	ACF	1st (Northern Ireland) Battalion ACF
SMI	J	KEENAN	ACF	1st Battalion The Highlanders ACF
SSI	F	THOMSON	ACF	1st Battalion The Highlanders ACF
SMI	E	MILLS	ACF	1st Battalion The Highlanders ACF
SSI	H	PORTER	ACF	2nd Battalion The Highlanders ACF
SSI	W	REED	ACF	Angus & Dundee Battalion ACF
Lt Col	S	HIGH	ACF	Angus & Dundee Battalion ACF
SSI	W	MCINTOSH	ACF	Argyll & Sutherland Highlanders Battalion ACF
SSI	D	NAISMITH	ACF	Argyll & Sutherland Highlanders Battalion ACF
Lt Col	C	CONNOR	CCF	Barnard Castle School CCF
SSI	P	SHILLINGFORD	ACF	Bedfordshire & Hertfordshire ACF
Capt	K	MARSHALLSAY	ACF	Bedfordshire & Hertfordshire ACF
SMI	A	PALFREMAN	ACF	Bedfordshire & Hertfordshire ACF
SMI	S	RENDALL	ACF	Bedfordshire & Hertfordshire ACF
Maj	A	LEE	ACF	Buckinghamshire (The Rifles) ACF
SMI	E	MATTHEWS	ACF	Buckinghamshire (The Rifles) ACF
Maj	R	MCALINDEN	ACF	Cambridgeshire ACF
SSI	H	TWIGG	ACF	City of London & North East Sector ACF
Lt	R	WALTON	ACF	City of London & North East Sector ACF
SI	A	RICHARDSON	ACF	Cleveland ACF
SMI	C	WILKINSON	ACF	Cleveland ACF
Maj	S	TURNER	ACF	Cleveland ACF
2Lt	B	REID	ACF	Clwyd & Gwynedd ACF
CF3	I E	JONES	ACF	Clwyd & Gwynedd ACF
Lt	D	JONES	ACF	Clwyd & Gwynedd ACF
Capt	D	JONES	ACF	Clwyd & Gwynedd ACF
Maj	M	AMBROSE	ACF	Cornwall ACF (The Rifles)
2Lt	B	OSBORNE	ACF	Cornwall ACF (The Rifles)
SMI	D	HEATHCOTE	ACF	Cornwall ACF (The Rifles)
Capt	D	YEOMANS	ACF	Cumbria ACF
Lt	I	STEWART	ACF	Devon ACF
SSI	A	LITTLEJOHNS	ACF	Devon ACF
SSI	A	SHORT	ACF	Dorset ACF

Rank	Initial	Surname	Org	Unit
Maj	J	STOCKFORD	ACF	Dorset ACF
SMI	C	JOYNES	ACF	Dorset ACF
Maj	G	BUCKELL	ACF	Essex ACF
Capt	N	WHARTON	CCF	Giggleswick School CCF
SSI	M	COBB	ACF	Glasgow & Lanarkshire Battalion ACF
SMI	M	SMILES	ACF	Gloucestershire ACF (The Rifles)
Lt	J	HARDING	ACF	Gloucestershire ACF (The Rifles)
SSI	M	PATTISON	ACF	Greater London South West Sector ACF
SMI	H	DAVIES	ACF	Gwent & Powys ACF
2Lt	JE	WRIGHT	ACF	Hampshire & Isle of Wight ACF
Lt	M	HOLDWAY	ACF	Hampshire & Isle of Wight ACF
Maj	A	TOZE	ACF	Hampshire & Isle of Wight ACF
SSI	P	WOLFE	ACF	Hampshire & Isle of Wight ACF
Maj	A	CHARANIA	CCF	Headington School CCF
Capt	J	HUCK	ACF	Hereford & Worcester ACF
SMI	M	TOWNLEY	ACF	Hereford & Worcester ACF
SMI	S	GRYNTUS	ACF	Hereford & Worcester ACF
Capt	J	EDWARDS	ACF	Hereford and Worcester ACF
Lt	E	FIELD	ACF	Humberside & South Yorkshire ACF
Capt	A	ROSS	CCF	Ipswich School CCF
Maj	S	TWYMAN	ACF	Kent ACF
Lt	T	YOUNG	ACF	Kent ACF
Capt	T	WORRALL	CCF	King Edward VI Grammar School (Chelmsford) CCF
Capt	P	DUNLOP	CCF	Kings School (Grantham) CCF
Lt	A	GILBERT	ACF	Leicestershire, Northamptonshire & Rutland ACF
SSI	G	SWIFT	ACF	Merseyside ACF
Maj	I	TYRER	ACF	Merseyside ACF
2Lt	A	ASHTON	ACF	Norfolk ACF
Capt	C	BRETT	ACF	Northumbria ACF
Col	S	KENDALL	ACF	Somerset Cadet Battalion (The Rifles) ACF
Col	R	SIMPKIN	ACF	Suffolk ACF
Capt	B	GERRARD	ACF	Suffolk ACF
Capt	C	MANSFIELD	ACF	Surrey ACF Battalion (PWRR)
SMI	P	SPOONER	ACF	Sussex ACF
Capt	N	BARTLETT	ACF	Sussex ACF
SSI	T	WILLIAMS	ACF	Sussex ACF
SMI	T	MCNAMARA	ACF	The West Lowland Battalion ACF
SMI	W	BOYD	ACF	The West Lowland Battalion ACF
SMI	R	BARKER	ACF	Warwickshire & West Midlands South Sector ACF
Capt	M	WILLIAMS	ACF	Warwickshire & West Midlands South Sector ACF
Maj	L	BAMPFIELD	ACF	Wiltshire ACF
SMI	K	COLLINS	ACF	Wiltshire ACF
Lt	D	NUTTALL	ACF	Yorkshire (North & West) ACF
SMI	R	GALLAGHER	ACF	Yorkshire (North & West) ACF

CADET FORCES MEDAL

Rank	Initial	Surname	Org	Unit
SSI	C	GREGG	ACF	1st (Northern Ireland) Battalion ACF
SI	J	BLAIR	ACF	1st (Northern Ireland) Battalion ACF
Col	A	DONALDSON	ACF	1st (Northern Ireland) Battalion ACF
SMI	I	MOAR	ACF	1st Battalion The Highlanders ACF
SSI	A	MCMAHON	ACF	1st Battalion The Highlanders ACF
SSI	A	NUGENT	ACF	2nd (Northern Ireland) Battalion ACF
SMI	N	GRIBBEN	ACF	2nd (Northern Ireland) Battalion ACF
SMI	K	WALKER	ACF	2nd Battalion The Highlanders ACF
SMI	G	CRUICKSHANK	ACF	2nd Battalion The Highlanders ACF
Capt	D	ACHESON	ACF	51X Non Effective Officers Pool
RSMI	C	SMITH	ACF	Argyll & Sutherland Highlanders Battalion ACF
Capt	H	FAIRWOOD	CCF	Barnard Castle School CCF
Maj	P	LAYCOCK	CCF	Batley Grammar School CCF
Capt	A	GANNON	ACF	Bedfordshire & Hertfordshire ACF
Capt	S	NORMAN	ACF	Bedfordshire & Hertfordshire ACF
SI	C V T	POTTS	ACF	Bedfordshire & Hertfordshire ACF
Maj	P	TURNER	ACF	Bedfordshire & Hertfordshire ACF
Capt	D	TAYLOR	ACF	Bedfordshire and Hertfordshire ACF
SMI	B	CLAY	ACF	Black Watch Battalion ACF
AUO	M L	RUSSELL	ACF	Black Watch Battalion ACF
Capt	T	CLINTON	CCF	Bromsgrove School CCF
Maj	J	FARNES	CCF	Bromsgrove School CCF
SMI	T	PROUT	ACF	Cambridgeshire ACF
SMI	E	BROOK	ACF	Cambridgeshire ACF
Capt	K	BLUNDELL	ACF	Cambridgeshire ACF
Lt Col	R	SUTHERLAND	ACF	Cambridgeshire ACF
SMI	N	WHITE	ACF	Cleveland ACF
SMI	K	BARRY	ACF	Cleveland ACF
SI	A	CALVERT	ACF	Cleveland ACF
Lt	R	NICHOLSON	ACF	Cleveland ACF
SMI	J	PALESCHI	ACF	Cleveland ACF
Capt	S	JUKES	ACF	Cleveland ACF
Maj	S	NORMAN	ACF	Cleveland ACF
Lt	L	DAVAGE	CCF	Clifton College CCF
2Lt	A	HUGHES	ACF	Clwyd & Gwynedd ACF
SI	C	BLACKWELL	ACF	Clwyd & Gwynedd ACF
SSI	K	MURRAY-JONES	ACF	Clwyd & Gwynedd ACF
AUO	G	WHITE	ACF	Cornwall ACF (The Rifles)
Lt	T	ATKINSON	CCF	Culford School CCF
Capt	S	FARRER	ACF	Cumbria ACF
SSI	D	FERGUSON	ACF	Cumbria ACF
SSI	C	LINDSLEY	ACF	Cumbria ACF
Lt	JL	ASHBURN	ACF	Derbyshire ACF (Mercian Regiment)
SMI	I	GOODMAN	ACF	Derbyshire ACF (Mercian Regiment)
SI	N	SLACK	ACF	Derbyshire ACF (Mercian Regiment)
SMI	H	ROGERS	ACF	Devon ACF
SMI	N	WEBSTER	ACF	Devon ACF
Capt	P	OSMASTON	ACF	Devon ACF
Maj	D	ABBOTT	ACF	Dorset ACF
SMI	P	RICHARDSON	ACF	Dorset ACF
SMI	L	TALBOT	ACF	Durham ACF
SMI	M	ROBERTS	ACF	Durham ACF
SI	D	GILLOTT	ACF	Durham ACF
Lt	M	TWIST	ACF	Durham ACF
Lt	J	NEWTON	CCF	Eastbourne College CCF
Lt	B	YERLI	ACF	Essex ACF
SMI	S	GALLEY	ACF	Essex ACF

Rank	Initials	Surname	Type	Unit
SSI	C	SOUTHGATE	ACF	Essex ACF
Lt	D	WASS	ACF	Essex ACF
Maj	C	PALMER	CCF	Felsted School CCF
SI	M	MCKEOWN	ACF	Glasgow & Lanarkshire Battalion ACF
CF3	E	SELEMANI	ACF	Glasgow & Lanarkshire Battalion ACF
Capt	S	JONES	ACF	Gloucestershire ACF (The Rifles)
Lt Col	A	AYRES	ACF	Gloucestershire ACF (The Rifles)
Maj	G	MILBURN	ACF	Greater London South East Sector ACF
Lt	A	MARTIN	ACF	Greater London South West Sector ACF
SI	S	HICKS	ACF	Greater London South West Sector ACF
SSI	J	QUILLIAM	ACF	Greater London South West Sector ACF
SMI	B	OVERINGTON	ACF	Greater London South West Sector ACF
CF3	P H	SUMSION	ACF	Greater Manchester ACF
SSI	D R	YOUNG	ACF	Greater Manchester ACF
Lt	P M	JACKSON	ACF	Greater Manchester ACF
Lt	S	HEARD	CCF	Haileybury College CCF
SSI	D	MARTIN	ACF	Hampshire & Isle of Wight ACF
SSI	S	RADFORD	ACF	Hampshire & Isle of Wight ACF
Lt	S	SLACK	ACF	Hampshire & Isle of Wight ACF
Lt	N	BLOY	ACF	Hampshire & Isle of Wight ACF
Maj	C	BILBOE	ACF	Hereford & Worcester ACF
SMI	W	ALLPORT	ACF	Hereford & Worcester ACF
RSMI	R	BILBOE	ACF	Hereford & Worcester ACF
2Lt	S	BARR	ACF	Humberside & South Yorkshire ACF
SI	D E	BURDETT	ACF	Humberside & South Yorkshire ACF
PI	J M	BRENTANO	ACF	Humberside & South Yorkshire ACF
Maj	M J	LUNDIE	ACF	Humberside & South Yorkshire ACF
SSI	J	COOPER-MORRIS	ACF	Kent ACF
SSI	M	BARTON	ACF	Kent ACF
SMI	P	EYLES	ACF	Kent ACF
SSI	I	BRIGHTMAN	ACF	Kent ACF
Capt	P	JONES	ACF	King Edward's School Bath CCF
SSI	N	WEBSTER	ACF	Lancashire ACF
SMI	R	METCALFE	ACF	Lancashire ACF
Lt	E	PINCOMBE-STRINGER	ACF	Leicestershire, Northamptonshire & Rutland ACF
SMI	J	THOMAS	ACF	Lincolnshire ACF
SMI	M L	FISHER	ACF	Lincolnshire ACF
Maj	J	FIELD	ACF	Lincolnshire ACF
SMI	M	PATON	ACF	Lincolnshire ACF
SSI	M	FLINDALL	ACF	Lincolnshire ACF
Lt Col	P	LAYCOCK	ACF	Lincolnshire ACF
Lt	D	MURPHY	CCF	Loughborough Grammar School CCF
Maj	C	NICHOLLS	CCF	Lucton School CCF
Lt Col	P	HIGHWAY	CCF	Maidstone Grammar School CCF
Lt	C	SEDDON	ACF	Merseyside ACF
SSI	T	PHILLIPS	ACF	Merseyside ACF
Lt	M J	DAVIES	ACF	Merseyside ACF
Capt	J	CRAWFORD	ACF	Merseyside ACF
SSI	D	ROSSITER	ACF	Merseyside ACF
SI	C	GIBSON	ACF	Merseyside ACF
SSI	G	GASSON	ACF	Middlesex & North West London Sector ACF
SMI	T	HENDERSON	ACF	Northumbria ACF
SI	C	HEALE	ACF	Northumbria ACF
Maj	T	TIDY	ACF	Nottinghamshire ACF
SMI	L	FIELDING	ACF	Nottinghamshire ACF
Capt	C	STANDLEY	CCF	Oundle School CCF
SSI	H	FOX	ACF	Oxfordshire (The Rifles) Battalion ACF
SSI	S	DOUGLAS-GILBERT	ACF	Oxfordshire (The Rifles) Battalion ACF
Capt	M	HAWKES	CCF	Plymouth College CCF
Maj	R	PASHA	CCF	Reading School CCF
Capt	K	PAUL	CCF	Robert Gordon's College CCF
SSI	R	YOUNG	ACF	Royal County of Berkshire ACF
SI	B	HABGOOD	ACF	Royal County of Berkshire ACF
SSI	J	SMITH	ACF	Royal County of Berkshire ACF
Capt	S	MCENDOO	ACF	Royal County of Berkshire ACF
SMI	A	MUGGERIDGE	ACF	Royal County of Berkshire ACF
CF3	C	HALL	ACF	Royal County of Berkshire ACF
SI	A	PETTET	ACF	Royal County of Berkshire ACF
SSI	A	MURPHY	ACF	Royal County of Berkshire ACF
SMI	L	GEORGE VAUGHAN	ACF	Royal County of Berkshire ACF
SSI	C	BLIGH	ACF	Shropshire ACF
SI	G	DAVIES-COWARD	ACF	Somerset Cadet Battalion (The Rifles) ACF
SSI	S	NAISH	ACF	Somerset Cadet Battalion (The Rifles) ACF
AUO	M	SKIDMORE	ACF	Somerset Cadet Battalion (The Rifles) ACF
Maj	C	JACKSON	CCF	St Columba's College CCF
SSI	S	DUNNING	ACF	Staffordshire & West Midlands North Sector ACF
Capt	J	MOODY	ACF	Staffordshire & West Midlands North Sector ACF
SSI	F	SMITH	ACF	Suffolk ACF
SMI	C	WILSON	ACF	Suffolk ACF
SMI	D	ROBINSON	ACF	Suffolk ACF
Maj	D	MASON	ACF	Suffolk ACF
SSI	M	EXLEY	ACF	Surrey ACF Battalion (PWRR)
SSI	M	ARROW	ACF	Surrey ACF Battalion (PWRR)
SSI	L	STOKES	ACF	Sussex ACF
Capt	J	FAWCETT	CCF	The Leys School CCF
SMI	J	MURPHY	ACF	The West Lowland Battalion ACF
SSI	P	MCINTYRE	ACF	The West Lowland Battalion ACF
Maj	A	HUXTER	CCF	Uppingham School CCF
2Lt	B	HAYWARD	ACF	Warwickshire & West Midlands South Sector ACF
SI	N	TAYLOR	ACF	Warwickshire & West Midlands South Sector ACF
SMI	R	KNIGHT	ACF	Warwickshire & West Midlands South Sector ACF
Maj	G	TAYLOR	ACF	Warwickshire & West Midlands South Sector ACF
SSI	V	RULE	ACF	Wiltshire ACF
SMI	B	WOODS	ACF	Wiltshire ACF
Capt	A	FINDLATER	ACF	Yorkshire (North & West) ACF
SI	J	FEARNLEY	ACF	Yorkshire (North & West) ACF
Lt	M	O'CONNOR	ACF	Yorkshire (North & West) ACF
SSI	R	COWARD	ACF	Yorkshire (North & West) ACF